Sharing Faith with Children

Also by Sara Covin Juengst
and published by Westminster/John Knox Press

Breaking Bread: The Spiritual Significance of Food

Sharing Faith with Children

Rethinking the Children's Sermon

Sara Covin Juengst

Westminster/John Knox Press
Louisville, Kentucky

Scripture quotations marked NRSV are from the New Revised Standard Version of the Bible, copyright © 1989 by the Division of Christian Education of the National Council of the Churches of Christ in the U.S.A., and are used by permission.

Scripture quotations marked TEV are from the *Good News Bible—Old Testament:* Copyright © American Bible Society 1976; *New Testament:* Copyright © American Bible Society 1966, 1971, 1976.

"Russian Orthodox Childhood," by Dee Horn, from *Alive Now* 18, no. 4 (July-August 1988): 60-61, is reprinted by permission of the author.

Book design by Carol Dukes Eberhart

Cover design by Kevin Darst, KDEE, Inc.

First edition

Published by Westminster/John Knox Press
Louisville, Kentucky

This book is printed on acid-free paper that meets the American National Standards Institute Z39.48 standard. ∞

PRINTED IN THE UNITED STATES OF AMERICA
9 8 7 6 5 4 3 2

Library of Congress Cataloging-in-Publication Data

Juengst, Sara Covin.
    Sharing faith with children : rethinking the children's sermon / Sara Covin Juengst — 1st ed.
            p.   cm.
    Includes bibliographical references.
    ISBN 0-664-25439-X
    1. Preaching to children.   2. Children—Religious life.
I. Title
BV4235.C4J84   1994
252'.53—dc20   93-31960

For Laura, Sara, Maggie, Adam, and Rachel

Contents

Foreword

"Do you do children's sermons?" asked the woman on the other end of the telephone line. I was scheduled to fill in as guest preacher and worship leader for her vacationing pastor the following Sunday, and she, as the chair of the worship committee, was calling to get the bulletin information and to complete the arrangements. "Time with the Children" was a regular part of their weekly worship, and she needed to know, among other things, if I was willing to take on this task in addition to the "regular" sermon. Since she did not know me, and sensing intuitively that this could be a touchy subject, she was cautious. "Do you do children's sermons?" she inquired warily.

She was right to ask, of course, and right to be cautious. Some preachers do children's sermons, and some don't. Both groups can advance serious-minded educational, liturgical, and theological arguments to justify their decisions, but mainly, I suspect, it boils down to comfort and fear. Some of us are comfortable with children, and some of us are not. Some of us warm instinctively to the children gathered around us, and some of us are afraid—afraid of what we don't know about the ways children think, afraid of appearing and sounding foolish, afraid of situations that can so easily slip out of control, afraid perhaps, of the children themselves.

In this volume, Sara Covin Juengst speaks to our fears.

She writes, of course, out of broad knowledge, discerning expertise, and deep experience, but mainly she speaks wisely and confidently in a voice that calms our anxieties. She teaches us about children—what they think and feel and need. She teaches us about ministry—how important what we do and say can be for a child. And she teaches us about preaching—how strong sermons grow out of scripture and articulate the good news to everyone, children and adults.

"Do you do children's sermons?" the woman wondered. If I had answered with complete candor, I would have replied, "Yes, I do children's sermons, but not very well." As is the case with many preachers, my training and experience have been so focused upon adults, I simply have not given sufficient attention to the particular needs and capacities of children. Not opposed in principle to the practice of children's sermons, I still lack the knowledge and skill to feel confident. Here, too, this book is of great value. Not only does it address our fears, it sharpens our skills. Not only is this book grounded in well-researched data regarding the emotional, cognitive, and spiritual development of children, it is an immensely practical work as well. Sara Covin Juengst patiently guides us through the educational and communicational theories of human development to the place where she can name clear and cogent guidelines for the creation of faithful messages for children.

What Sara Covin Juengst has written in these pages is a wonderful gift to all preachers. Because of the insights gathered and developed here, the next time we are asked, "Do you do children's sermons?" we are far more likely to be able to respond with a firm and bold, "Yes!"

Thomas G. Long

Princeton Theological Seminary

Preface

This book is for anyone who faces the task of preparing a children's sermon with dread, reluctance, or a "blank slate" mind. It is designed to provide practical information and suggestions for making this part of the worship service a meaningful experience for children and a joy for sermon-givers.

It was born out of my love for children—as pastor, teacher, friend, mother, and grandmother. I have listened to children and shared the faith with them for almost five decades. If I have any wisdom on the subject to offer, it is because of what they have taught me.

I have always enjoyed telling stories to children, but I have become aware in recent years that there are many for whom it is an uncomfortable experience. This book seeks to provide some psychological, theological, and educational information that will make this time for sharing the faith with children become richer, deeper, and, perhaps, even a moment of awe and wonder.

S.C.J.

ONE

The Children's Sermon, Burden or Blessing?

Emil Nolde's painting *Jesus and the Children* shows Jesus embracing several children who are wreathed in light, while the adult disciples look on from the shadowy periphery, not quite trusting what is going on, not quite sure of the propriety of the situation, not quite certain the children are worth so much of the Master's time and energy. Their scowls communicate the question: Why bother with children?

This painting could serve as a paradigm of what happens in those moments which, with increasing frequency, are especially set aside for children in worship services. The text upon which the painting is based (Matt. 19:13–15) is the one most often called upon by those who wish to justify these set-apart moments, especially when they take the form of a children's sermon or "message." It is a text that certainly leaves little room for doubt about the importance of children to our Lord.

However, Nolde's painting also captures some of the many levels of doubt and controversy that today surround these seemingly innocent moments in worship. The adults in the congregation who look on are not always quite sure what should be taking place. While some are content to be entertained, others wonder about its propriety. Educators have grave doubts about what is actually happening from a liturgical, educational, and theological perspective. Some ministers are not really convinced that designing a message just for children deserves any real expenditure of time and energy. And many of us find ourselves watching from the shadows with detachment, skepticism, boredom, or even annoyance and frustration.

The confusion about what this time ought to be is reflected in the many names given to it: "Children's Sermon," "Children's Message," "Time for the Children," "Moments with the Children," "A Word About Worship," and even "The Pastor's Pals." Perhaps no other part of the contemporary worship service is the subject of so much debate. And even when there is a belief in the importance of the children's sermon, many sermon-givers face it with attitudes of quiet desperation.

As an educator, I have felt frustrated listening to pastors and lay people struggling to make this small interlude a meaningful part of the worship service for young children. I have heard poor theology, inappropriate language, pious moralisms, absurd analogies, and, worst of all, the reduction of the gospel message to trivialities so banal that even the children are bored. What is wrong? I asked myself. Why is it that otherwise competent, intelligent ministers and lay people become woefully inadequate when it comes to sharing the good news with God's little ones? Over and over again I have heard an undercurrent of pain and desperation from those who struggle each Sunday to find some good words to say to the children of the congregation.

Is it worth the trouble to try? Is the children's sermon worthy of preservation? Can its use be justified as good liturgy and sound educational practice? I believe it can, but as an educator I am also convinced that it takes preparation. I believe it is very important to know how young children think and feel before we begin the task of trying to communicate with them about faith. I believe it is helpful to gain some perspective on what scholars have discovered about how that faith develops in early childhood and how children express their spiritual needs. In addition, I believe it is vitally necessary to know how to use the tools of language and symbolism, of image and story, as we attempt to translate abstract theological concepts into a child's daily experience. All this will help those of us who love children to find better ways to proclaim the gospel of Jesus Christ to them. I am convinced that, when properly done, the children's sermon can be an instrument of that proclamation.

It goes without saying that many of the criticisms leveled at children's sermons are justifiable. Alan Smith has helpfully categorized these criticisms into three groups. There are educational concerns: too much emphasis on the cognitive, the intellectual, and the verbal; a lack of integrity; and moralisms, legalisms, and the use of abstract concepts. Theological concerns include a focus on the child rather than on God, manipulation of biblical texts, the unrelatedness of the children's sermon to the rest of worship, and the implication that the sermon-giver has all the answers. Finally, Smith lists what he describes as inclusion/exclusion considerations: an emphasis on the individual rather than the corporate nature of the church, the implication that the "real" sermon is just for adults, and the exclusion of the rest of the congregation from this time "just for the children."[1]

These are all valid criticisms, but those who share faith with children do not have to suffer any of these pitfalls. It is my firm belief that, with proper thought and care, this special time with children can be a rich and beautiful experience.

In the following chapters attention will be given to the meaning of worship and how children participate in it, the role and purpose of the children's message, the psychological and theological developmental processes of young children, the use of language and symbolism with children, and the appropriate methodologies that will help us in our efforts to share the faith with children through that instrument of proclamation, the children's sermon.

TWO

The Worship Setting

It is a pleasant tableau—the little ones gathered on the chancel steps, the congregation looking on with amusement and pleasure at their innocent faces, and the minister smiling beneficently. What could possibly be wrong with such a charming scene? The minister likes it, the congregation likes it, and the children like it. But educators and theologians have, as we have already seen, raised some serious objections to this seemingly innocuous addition to the liturgy, the children's sermon. In the first chapter, we looked at some of the questions that have been raised about its intrinsic worth, its educational value, its appropriateness for young children, and its methodology. We will examine all these issues in subsequent chapters. But the basic issue is a theological and liturgical one. Before we can decide if the children's sermon is appropriate, we must take a serious look at its context: the worship setting.

Two personal experiences may highlight what worship can mean to children.

The first occurred in an Orthodox church in Moscow. The church was a visual feast: frescoes of biblical scenes, the gold-encrusted icons, a soft glow of candles. Everywhere one looked were symbolic reminders of the gospel message. It was also an auditory feast: the hidden choir somewhere above and behind sounded truly like the voices of angels. The music flowed effortlessly from the choir to the priests, and from the priests to the congregation, unbroken by prosaic announcements of hymn numbers. There was constant movement: priests gliding through the intricate choreography of the liturgy, faithful women caring for their church by bustling about to scoop up the tallow falling from the flickering candles, worshipers quietly slipping aside to pray before the icons, and, in a climactic moment, the entire congregation in a reverent hush, moving toward the priests to receive Holy Communion. In the middle of the crowd of worshipers was a father holding his small son in his arms. Not once in the two-hour service did the small child seem restless or bored. Instead, he was lost in wonder: at the beauty, the sound, the press of the eager worshipers. The experience had captured him totally. He was enthralled.

That moment shows something about the nature of worship that makes a lasting impression. It shows a community, caught up in the awe and wonder of God's goodness, entering so wholeheartedly into praise of that goodness that time became meaningless. No one was watching the clock. And in the midst was a young child, also caught up in awe and wonder. This does not imply that the child's cognitive understanding was complete. His fascination may have been similar to the fascination children have with the marvels of Walt Disney World or our Fourth of July fireworks. But in a community of adults who were passionate about their worship, in a ceremony where visual and auditory impact heightened the atmosphere of mystery and transcendence, he could not help but experience some of the essentials of true worship.

Dee Horn verifies this in her own poetic reminiscence, "Russian Orthodox Childhood":[1]

> I was young.
> I noticed first the smells—
> the smoke from candles

the incense puffs
and the lingering gifts
of a taste of wine.

Then an uncommon man in a full-length gown
going up and down the holy steps.
The rest of us were enthroned on knees.
(Or were lying down.)
Then the soothing chants.
And the body swirls.
The lamp of fire.
And the way adults
would concentrate
on doing all just right.

No one had to say not to laugh or run
or play a game of tag.
It was our choice to sit quite still and swallow life
as a mystery.

I was very young.
But I can close my eyes and see it yet.
And my now-deaf ears still hear the bells.
Yet when I look it up in a formal book
to see what they say of words like this:
Russian Orthodox Christians
What they say in a page or a paragraph
doesn't seem like a room of candlelight
and words from God.
I read the facts, but the facts fail to smell.
The printed type is accurate,
but doesn't cling
like memory's scenes.

Now that I've grown old,
those scenes are fat—
they've enlarged at the end of each year.

Perhaps they lie—
or at least fudge the truth.
Perhaps they're the dream of a child.

Can life last beyond the everyday?
Can the world say more than the words we use?
Can chants while kneeling hold it all?
It's hard to say.
But something there must have been done right,
If all it takes in my life today
is burning candles and incense smell
    to have me know to worship God.

The setting for the second experience is quite different: a small rural church in South Carolina. The attendance record on the wall noted that there had been eleven present at Sunday school that morning. The occasion was the annual Christmas program, to be highlighted by the children's reenactment of the nativity scene. Three small congregations had gathered for this occasion, so the little brick church was comfortably full. Poinsettias, greenery, candles, a small Chrismon tree, and an advent wreath brightened the rather spartan sanctuary. There were not many children in these church memberships, so there were only one wise man and one shepherd. But the magic was there, in two-and-a-half-year-old Matthew, in his shepherd garb. Matthew was a child of this church. From the first week of his life, he had occupied his parents' pew along with his brothers, David and Jonathan. The congregation had watched the boys grow, had seen them every Sunday shyly gathering in the front row when the minister called out, "Where are my young ones?" Only recently had Matthew felt secure enough to leave the safe haven of his father's arms to join the rest of the children up front for the children's sermon. But it was little Matthew, child of the covenant, whose voice rang out above all the rest, singing "Hark, the Herald Angels Sing." It was the wide-eyed wonderment in his eyes as he stood next to his brothers that proved Matthew knew what awe and holiness are all about. It was Matthew's presence there, in the church where his father and mother and grandmother worshiped, that showed again what ritual really is: a remembering, a reenactment by a community of the truths that hold the community together. In that little brick church, the Christ was truly born again. In the shining eyes of Matthew was the light of a star.

In both these examples, children were a part of the whole worship service. Ideally, this is the way it should be. The sermon, the music, the prayers, the scripture reading—all should address children as well as adults. Many books provide ideas on how to achieve this ideal goal. Among them are David Ng and Virginia Thomas's *Children in the Worshiping Community* and Margie Morris's *Helping Children Feel at Home in Church*. Morris admits, however, that it is not easy to incorporate children into the whole liturgy, especially when it comes to giving them leadership roles. Concerns arise about loss of dignity, about making children into "performers," about losing the "traditional" and familiar worship format (the "we've never done it that way" syndrome). Other concerns have to do with the restlessness of young children during an hour-long service and the attendant uneasiness of parents.

The reality is that, in most churches, children are not included in the whole of the service, and most special attention to them comes by means of the children's sermon. Children's sermons are not going to go away any time soon. The question is, How do we use this special but limited instrument of proclamation with integrity as we seek to incorporate children into the worship life of the congregation?

If we are serious about what happens to our children in the worshiping community, perhaps it will be helpful to think about what we can learn about worship from those little ones in Moscow and South Carolina.

What Is Worship?

Scholars both secular and religious have struggled for years to define worship and to determine why it seems to be an essential human need. Here are some of their definitions.

"Worship is . . . response to the greatness and goodness of God . . . the central act of the Christian life, empowering and ennobling all else that constitutes Christian living."[2]

"Worship is the celebrative response to what God has done, is doing, and promises to do."[3]

"[Worship is] the deliberate act of seeking to approach reality at its deepest level by becoming aware of God in and through Jesus Christ and by responding to this awareness."[4]

"Worship is both an intellectual and an emotional activity, and the Spirit moves amidst the process to bind the community to one another and to God."[5]

"Participation in worship is primarily for the purpose of praising God rather than of being personally inspired."[6]

Worship as Response

A key element in these definitions is response. If it is true that worship is response, there must be something to which we are responding. John Burkhart identifies it with the words "what God has done, is doing, and promises to do." God has acted: creating, redeeming, forgiving, restoring. It is in response to God's abounding grace that we worship. The word used most often in the New Testament for worship is *proskyneo*, which literally means "kissing the ground before a deity." Although this expression is not used in the New Testament in connection with community worship, it is frequently used to denote awe, reverence, and wonder, as when the wise men "knelt down and paid him homage" (Matt. 2:11, NRSV). This kind of awe is experienced in the presence of kings and monarchs as well as before manifestations of the holy.

True liturgy starts by addressing God in praise and thanksgiving. In the very act of responding to God, we are given a new orientation that enables us to face the realities of life.

Burkhart helpfully identifies the three dimensions of worship as "acknowledgment, rehearsal, and proclamation." Acknowledgment is not only knowing cognitively that God is real but making an affirmative response to that reality by living a certain way. Rehearsal implies a place where we practice our parts in God's drama. As Burkhart puts it, "Responsible worship rehearses graced reality."[7] The test of the effectiveness of the rehearsal is whether lives are transformed in the process. Worship as proclamation is a way of telling the world what God "has done, is doing, and promises to do." We respond to the good news by proclaiming our experience of it to the rest of the world through the open witness of our worship.

Are children capable of making these responses of acknowledgment, rehearsal, and proclamation? In his book *The Spiritual Life of Children*, Robert Coles, a noted child psychiatrist, makes the point that it is very difficult to measure children's spiritual understanding. His method of interviewing children about their religious lives involved staying with a number of children long enough to earn their trust and learn from them. He found that the questions asked by Gauguin just before he died ("Where do we come from? What are we? Where are we going?") are the questions children ask "more intensely, unremittingly, and subtly than we sometimes imagine." He quotes Tommy, a fourth grader: "You have to trust in God when you try to imagine Him."[8]

In spite of the difficulty of interviewing children and measuring their capacity for spiritual understanding, it seems evident that there are many special moments in children's experiences that serve as turning points. Although it is hard for children to describe what is happening, many adults in reflecting on these moments identify them as deeply spiritual experiences. A remarkable book by Edward Robinson, *The Original Vision*, records many such moments. For example:

> As a small child one of my favorite festivals was Trinity Sunday. It seemed to me quiet and beautiful, and happening about midsummer became associated in my mind with green trees and flowers in bloom. It was "mysterious" and right, something far bigger than the words used in church about it which sounded to a small child nonsense. But Trinity wasn't nonsense, it was Holy, holy, holy, as we sang in the hymn, and even a very young child could join in a sort of "oneness" with all things bright and beautiful and worship this Something so great and lovely that it didn't matter at all that it was also not understood. It just *was*.[9]

This vision records a child's acknowledgment of the *mysterium tremendum*, of the "holy other," of "graced reality." It is just such perceptions that give meaning to life and are the touchstones to transformation. Without knowing it, the child was rehearsing a part in "God's drama" through the medium of worship. The act of worship offered him a language, a way to speak the ineffable and indescribable, the dim perception of something "great and lovely," and therefore became, for the child, a vehicle for proclamation as well.

The mother of one four-year-old wrote down his prayer after moving to a new home. The prayer illustrates that it *is* possible for children to make a response in worship to their recognition of God's love and care. Jimmy prayed:

> Dear God,
> Thank you for your wonderful world!
> There's so much people—more than I can count!
> I just make more friends and more friends.
> Thank you for all the boys and girls in my class.
> And help the sick boys and girls.

And thank you for the moving van that came
here as quick as it could.
And for Grandma fixing Mother's chairs—they
look so nice!
Thank you, God, for everything. Amen.

Worship as Gathering

Although the worship experience is intensely personal, it comes to its fullness only in community. It is worship that gives meaning to the church. In the words of Paul Vieth, it is "at the heart of what the church is and does."[10] The Greek word *ekklesia*, which we generally translate "church," literally means a gathering or assembly. It is a community gathered together by God to learn what it means to be the people of God. As the community gathers, it expresses its response to God in worship. Because of the centrality of worship in the life of the gathered community, it has a responsibility to understand what worship is and what constitutes an appropriate liturgy.

What happens in congregational worship that does not happen in church school or in the home? What is communicated about faith that cannot be communicated elsewhere? James Carr says it is "the shared ecology of faith consciousness within the wider boundaries of the Christian community."[11] I like that image. A child who is immersed in nature, who stands with arms outspread to fields, trees, the sky, the clouds, has a different ecological understanding of nature from a child who lives in a city tenement and knows about fields and trees only from pictures in a book. Something happens in the immediacy of the immersion experience that makes a lasting impression. I still carry in my heart scenes from my own childhood of pastures and pine trees, of lying on my back to watch the lazy clouds, of the lacy fans of pecan leaves against a deep-blue southern sky. Carr is saying that it is important for the children's sermon to be a part of the ecology of Christian worship, with its wide range of sights, sounds, movements, and smells, so that similar lasting impressions can be formed for the child. It is this "shared ecology of consciousness" that the Russian child and little Matthew were experiencing, as colors, sounds, movements, and smells washed over them in their very different worship settings.

This "shared ecology of faith consciousness" has also to do with the feeling of belonging, of being cared about, of having a place, a family, of being loved and known by name. It is a powerful experience for children to be part of a worshiping community of adults who are acknowledging that there is something greater than they are.

Iris Cully says the same thing in different words:

> The church at worship is a people who believe in God and assume that [God] is in their midst. This assurance is carried to the child, who responds to what [is sensed] in the adults. It needs no verbal explanation. The nature of the understanding of God is made clear when joy, praise, and thanksgiving predominate.[12]

Worship as Choreography

It is not a frivolous thing, this turning our minds and hearts to God. It is tragic that we can so quickly lose the mystery and awe in our pettiness over details. Communing with God evaporates in our criticisms of the choir or the sermon. Even the liturgy becomes a distraction if it is unfamiliar. It takes discipline and understanding to look beyond the format to the deeper levels of meaning in worship. The Directory for Worship of the Presbyterian Church (U.S.A.) recognizes the need for congregational education about worship in order to reach these levels and suggests that the session provide for this education "by means appropriate to the age, interests, and circumstances of the members of the congregation."[13]

What are these deeper levels of meaning? Why do people

worship? The answer lies in our needs: our need for a set time and place for gathering with others to consider what God has done for us and to respond with praise and adoration, our need for the strength and support of other Christians, our need for a familiar ritual or liturgy, and our need to confess our sense of personal inadequacy and find forgiveness and renewal. The liturgy gathers up all these needs and provides a vehicle by which the community can express its corporate longings and joys. As such, it must be inclusive. It must find a way to make everyone—male or female, young or old, learned or uneducated, strong or disabled—feel that it is for them and expresses their deepest needs.

In order for this to happen, worship must be carefully prepared. It must have unity, design, movement, rhythm—in short, choreography. All of us who admired the dancing of Fred Astaire and Ginger Rogers through the last few decades are aware of the careful planning that lay behind their seemingly artless footwork. Preparation is essential for the faultless execution of their dances. In the same way, preparation for worship is almost as important as the liturgy itself.

Ritual is the choreography of worship, carefully polished by generations of the faithful into formats that provide times for adoration, confession, thanksgiving, and supplication. When new elements such as a children's sermon are added to age-old formulas, they must be carefully examined to see if they are in step with the choreography of the whole.

The choreography of worship is expressed in symbolic acts. Ritual is a way of saying things that need expression in ways other than words. Through symbolic acts we celebrate what is vitally important to us. We act out our response to what God has done for us and, in so doing, find ourselves reoriented to what life is all about. Burkhart claims that ritual should be "festive, sometimes almost playful, conspicuous in its gladness . . . its sounds are holy glee."[14] If this is true, children are ideally equipped both to participate in and to appreciate good liturgy. Their playfulness, their imagination, and their untarnished sense of wonder all put them ahead of the rest of us in the ability to respond unreservedly to the marvel of God's love.

Worship as Wonder

What is it that makes an experience religious? As theologians have tried to define what is essentially indefinable, they have used words such as "a sense of the mystery of being" or "a numinous sense of the presence of God." Perhaps we could say that the essence of a religious experience is that it helps us make sense of life by giving us an awareness of a different order of reality. It is an experience of awe and wonder that drives us to our knees in praise and adoration. It can be mysterious, awesome, joyful, calm, serene, and peaceful or frightening, lonely, and disturbing. It can be an experience of pleasure and ecstasy or of melancholy and longing. It makes us say yes to life, because it restores in us a sense of balance and harmony. We find ourselves murmuring, "This is what it's all about."

Sofia Cavalletti says that wonder is connected with going deeply into reality "because if we skim over things we will never be surprised by them."[15]

It is these experiences that form our religious attitudes. They are the crucial foundation to our doctrinal expressions. Without them, our cognitive understanding is dry and static. Children can and do have these experiences, although they are limited in their ability to describe what they are feeling. We must read it in their eyes. As we have seen, the attitudes that lead to worship are inherent in children. Edward Robinson records many examples of children's early experiences of awe and wonder. Here are some samples:

> I remember very clearly from the years before I was nine listening very carefully to the words in the Litany and to the Responses of the Congregation, and being

very much awed by what seemed to me to be tremendous words. Everyone seemed to me to mean what they were saying.[16]

The beauty of the cathedrals and churches, the mystery of the ritual, the rich pageantry and above all the appeal of the glorious sound of music and even of church bells, all combined to strengthen a sense of awe and reverence which I was familiar with in nature. Although I was rather a solitary child, it felt good to be part of a large worshiping community who acknowledged the presence of something greater than themselves.[17]

These childhood moments of wonder and transcendence are representative of the "shared ecology of faith consciousness" described by James A. Carr, which goes beyond cognitive understanding. Such moments are crucial because they are the seedbeds of committed faith. If children's sermons do nothing more than create moments of awe and wonder, characterized by a genuine sense of praise and thanksgiving, they are indeed instruments of proclamation.

Children and Sacraments

The sacraments are ideal moments for leading children to experience that awe and wonder which we have identified as important components of worship. Like all symbols, they are multivalent: that is, their power to communicate truth has many levels. They teach, of course, but they do more than that. They provide opportunities for rehearsing or reenacting the basic theological understandings of our Christian faith. We participate in those acts and, in the process, internalize their meanings even before we are aware of what is happening. It is because they are primarily affective rather than cognitive confrontations that our imaginations are stirred so deeply.

Children, who learn first through feelings and emotions, can be drawn into the mystery of the sacraments. Later, this experience will be the foundation for a more fully developed cognitive understanding of what is taking place.

We have already stated that children need to have a sense of belonging, of being claimed. Baptism is the rite in which that belonging is affirmed. It celebrates becoming part of the family of God. With each baptism, there is an opportunity to reaffirm this sense of belonging for all of us.

Although not all communions admit children to the Lord's Table, it is still possible for children to be caught up in the drama of the meal and the ceremony even if they are observers and not actual participants. It is an impressive visual teaching, and although it helps when children understand what is happening, much is communicated to them in the atmosphere of praise and prayer that accompanies the Supper. It can be a deeply felt experience in the presence of an understanding community.

Children and the Liturgical Seasons

The liturgical year, with its colors, symbols, and thematic emphases, offers many opportunities for engaging children in worship visually and emotionally. The emphases of each season can form the basis for children's sermons. Excellent examples are found in *Let All the People* by Agnes Junkin Peery. Paul Larose's *Working with Children and the Liturgy* and Karen Leslie's *Faith and Little Children* provide many ideas for children's sermons based on the liturgical year. Judy Gattis Smith also offers seasonal emphases in her book of children's liturgies, *Come, Children, Praise and Play.*

Christmas is probably the most meaningful festival of the church year for young children. It is easy to interpret Christmas as Jesus' birthday and to emphasize the joy of that occasion. Children love to hear or dramatize the Christmas story, sing the Christmas songs, and talk about Jesus as a baby whose birthday has become a time of love and giving. It is more difficult for young children to make the connection of the Christ child with the adult Jesus, but it is important to help them do so.

Even very young children can understand that we show our love for Jesus on his birthday by giving gifts to others, both at home and at church. My daughter-in-law wanted to teach this concept to her four-year-old by helping her buy a toy to give to a poor child. The problem was that little Maggie, having had no experience of poverty, could not imagine a child being without toys. Christmas gift-giving gave her a new perspective on the world and broadened her compassion for those less fortunate.

The chief difficulty with Christmas is how to prevent the Santa Claus story from obscuring the central figure of Jesus in Christmas celebrations. This presents a particular challenge for children's sermon-givers on the Sunday after Christmas, when children's minds are full of "what Santa brought."

The Easter message is more difficult to convey to young children, but since it is central to Christian thought and life, it is important to share it with even the youngest member of the congregation. We want the child's joy to be more than the experience of Easter eggs and bunnies. The story of Jesus' death is not easy for children to understand. The mother of four-year-old Lee was worried because Lee was obsessed with drawing pictures of Jesus on the cross for several weeks after Easter. He was apparently trying to work out his confusion about the event through the medium of art. Although we would like to shield children from the sadness of Jesus' suffering and death, it is impossible to do so. The best approach is to present the basic ideas by telling the story in broad outline, not by elaborating the suffering of Christ but by stressing the Easter joy of Jesus' friends, who were glad he was with them again.

Easter is a special day for remembering Jesus, but it is also a day of joy because of the return of spring. In our children's sermons, we can help children begin to understand that the new life we see in the world of nature reminds us that Jesus, too, was dead and is alive again. Traditional Easter customs need to be dealt with as carefully as we do the Santa Claus story. It is easy for children to see how buds and springtime blossoms remind us of new life, but Easter bunnies should be minimized and treated simply as a fun sort of make-believe. Be careful about the use of the butterfly as an Easter symbol. One minister explained that "because the butterfly dies, goes into a cocoon (which is like a tomb), and then comes out in the spring bringing us a great deal of joy, it is an appropriate symbol for Easter." This is far too difficult an analogy for young children, especially since it is the caterpillar who goes into the cocoon, and it does not actually die. It is better to say simply that the butterfly coming out of the cocoon reminds us how Jesus came out of the tomb and is alive.

To summarize, children are ready to worship. They are ready to "acknowledge, rehearse and proclaim" with the gathered community. Their wonderful openness, their colorful imaginations, and their sense of wonder all combine to put them in a state of readiness for worship. Our problem has been that we have insisted on treating them like little adults. Can we instead learn how to open the gates of awe and wonder for these little ones on their terms and in their language? It is both an awesome task and a priceless opportunity.

THREE

The Sermon as Instrument of Proclamation

What is the role of the children's sermon? What potential does it have for enriching the liturgy? Are there certain clear arguments that we can make to justify its existence? How does it fit into the choreography of worship?

These are essential questions for us to answer if we want the children's sermon to be more than perfunctory or trite, if we want it to be an instrument of proclamation and a channel of awe and wonder. It is not enough to use it simply because it is the trend or because the adults in the congregation expect it. We need to think clearly about its potential and to understand what it can accomplish.

The key word that provides a raison d'être for the children's sermon is *belonging*. This is an important concept for them. There are at least four aspects of belonging that can be addressed in this special time with children.

Children Belong to God

This is a fundamental theological concept. The children's sermon provides an opportunity to affirm in a variety of ways that children are important to God, are "precious in God's sight," and are loved by God. The children hear this in other places, of course, but to hear it affirmed by a loving, caring adult in a place set aside for worship has the possibility of new levels of certainty and authority. Jesus affirmed this loving concern. The verb *enankalizesthai*, which literally means to hug, is used only twice in the New Testament (Mark 9:36 and 10:16), and both times it refers to children. It is used when Jesus blesses the children and when he describes discipleship by hugging a child and saying, "Whoever welcomes in my name one of these children, welcomes me" (Mark 9:37, TEV).

Jerry Marshall Jordan has expressed this concept well. "We begin by responding to the inquiring spirits of our children and in giving assurance that God seeks to be known even by the young in our care. . . . They need to know how to think and speak of God, which will in turn honor God and enhance life."[1]

The Word of God Belongs to Children

Eldon Weisheit points out that "it is not our generosity that moves us to do the work and provide the time for children's messages. What we have found in God's Word belongs to the children."[2]

Although sharing God's Word is an important element in our Sunday school and Bible school programs, we must not leave it up to them to do the job alone. The sharing of the Word in families plays a crucial role in a child's faith development, but it is also very important that the Word be shared with children in the corporate experience of the worshiping congregation. The children's sermon offers an opportunity for the Word to be heard in language and images children can understand. Stories from God's Word can be selected that communicate to children the loving presence of God, the reality of Jesus Christ, and the faith of biblical characters. Not every Bible story is appropriate for children's sermons, but it should be *the* basic resource from which the sermons are drawn. When biblical stories are used, the place where they are found should be indicated to the children, so a connection is made between the stories and the book.

Children Belong to the Body of Christ

The inclusion of a time for children in the order of worship says to the children, We have thought about you; we have included you; we care about you. Christian Education professor Iris Cully comments: "A church that ignores children, segregating them into Sunday school rooms, rarely making provision for them to be among adults, conditions them to feel unwanted."[3]

The children's sermon can help integrate children into the sacramental and ritual life of the community; they begin to learn its language and to feel at home with it, to become a part of it. They have the opportunity to experience the congregation as a community of caring people.

Robert Coles has spent thirty years writing about children in various parts of the world. After finishing his work *The Moral Life of Children,* he decided to investigate children and faith. His research took many years to complete and, as he says, helped him "see children as seekers, as young pilgrims well aware that life is a finite journey and as anxious to make sense of it as those of us who are farther along in the time allotted to us."[4] The result was his significant work *The Spiritual Life of Children,* which shows that the importance of religious feelings in the early years cannot be overestimated. The impressions made upon children in rituals, worship, and the celebration of religious customs are lasting.

There is another aspect to this belonging: It provides an opportunity for the congregation to learn from the children. In a spontaneous postscript to a children's sermon, a minister added these touching words: "You teach us, the adults, things and we listen." It was good for both the congregation and the children to have this truth affirmed. John Westerhoff says, "Our question ought never be, How can we make our children into Christians? Rather, it must be, How can we *be* Christians with our children?"[5] Being with children in worship reminds us of the child in us. The wistful eagerness in adult faces as they watch children gathering for their sermon is a nostalgia for something that has been lost: an innocence, an openness, even a vulnerability.

Although it should never be forgotten that the children's sermon is for children and is not an undercover way to get at the adults, it is undeniably true that adults hear it and learn from it as well. This is not at all bad. In fact, it has something to do with the fact that good children's messages are simple, clear, focused, and concrete and deal with the basics of the faith. Too much of "adult" sermonizing is so heavily abstract that the Word is lost in words. The return to primary affections, basic symbols, and elementary concepts can be enriching.

The physical gathering of the children has another valid function. It serves as a visual reminder to the faith community of its responsibility for its baptized children; the fact of their *belonging* means they need care, guidance, and nurture from the community. One young minister tells of the first Sunday he tried a children's sermon. As he called for the children to come forward, he was aware of disapproval on the faces of some of the older members. But as the children came, and came, and continued to come until about sixty of them were gathered at the front of the church, the disapproval turned to sheer amazement. Few adults had had any idea there were so many children present! We need visible reminders of the whole body of Christ.

The church, like any other family, needs people of all ages. It needs the elderly, the middle-aged, young adults, children, and youth. All learn the meaning of Christian concern through their interaction. Parents feel welcomed along with their children. Within the church family, as in any other, it is important that people be sensitive to one another. There are times for young and old to be apart and times for them to be together. The worship service is one of those times when all ages should meet and be aware of one another's presence, even if only for a short while. The adage "Out of sight, out of mind" contains truth. When adults never see the young children that are a part of the family, they tend to forget them and their needs. The church needs to stay alert to the task of being the body of Christ and nurturing its baptized members.

As Eldon Weisheit phrases it:

> Children are a part of the church. Children in a worship service are not like uninvited offspring who gatecrash a wedding reception. They are not brought along to church only because the parents couldn't find or afford a baby-sitter. . . . Using children's messages is one way to help children feel they are a part of the body of believers—and also a way for adults to recognize children as their brothers and sisters in Christ.[6]

The Minister Also Belongs to the Children

As I have interviewed ministers about the benefits of the children's sermon, most comment on the special feeling of closeness that develops between pastor and children. The sermon provides an opportunity for warmth and intimacy that is very precious indeed. It affirms to the children that the minister, a figure of central importance in the church, cares about them, finds them interesting, and is willing to literally come down to their level, to be with them rather than tower over them from behind an awesome pulpit. In short, the minister becomes a human being rather than a godlike apparition who is unapproachable.

Brant Baker says, "What the children's sermon provides is an opportunity for children to be loved by an adult in an intentional way, not through some incidental time in worship, but through an *incarnational reality* that creates love, understanding, and belonging."[7] The warmth and easy interaction of children with the minister is an important part of this experience, and can even compensate in many ways for the dangers mentioned in chapter 1: language that is too abstract or a fuzzily conceived moral lesson. For example, in a small rural church where there are only five children in the congregation, there is normally no hesitation when the pastor asks for the "young people" to come down front. But on one occasion, two-year-old Matthew hung back. His father took him by the hand and led him up to the minister, who picked him up, saying, "Here's my friend, Matthew. Matthew, I remember when you were just a baby and your parents brought you to church. And I remember when you got bigger and could come down front with your brothers. I've watched you grow, and I've watched your brothers grow. And so have all those people out there. We are your family, Matthew." I don't remember what the rest of the children's sermon was that day, and Matthew probably doesn't either. But he won't forget the love and care expressed in those few words and in that hug he received.

Obviously, this is easier for some people than for others. Some adults feel quite comfortable with children, and others are afraid they won't know what to say. Children are very perceptive and generally know when an adult is ill at ease with them. They respond well to warmth, sincerity, and calmness. They are quick to sense phony heartiness and will become bored or restless if an adult is aloof or cold. Clergy often seem forbidding to children, or at the very least slightly bigger than life. It's not uncommon for very young children to confuse the minister with God. This awesomeness can be alleviated if the minister sits on the level of the children and is "touchable."

There's another important aspect of this opportunity for a close relationship with the minister. It gives the children who are not present for the rest of the worship service an opportunity to see the minister function in a preaching role addressed to them. When the minister does this in an effective way, it can provide a transition to the time when they will hear the word of God taught through adult sermons. Margie Morris points out that if every child had other chances to get to know the pastor, or if children were naturally integrated into the service as leaders and participants, we could dispense with the children's sermon, but until then, she says, "many parents are glad that caring pastors are reaching out to children and that the children are finding their way into cleric laps to receive the message."[8]

When the minister is the one participating in this time with the children, it is easier for their message to be correlated with the other parts of the service, especially the scripture and the sermon. The result is a cohesive unity in the liturgy, so that the children's sermon is not a time-out, or an interruption, but is integrally related to the whole. This is part of the choreography of worship. In many cases, the children's sermon can be drawn from the adult sermon's text, or it may be a rephrasing in children's terms of the sermon's main point. It may also be based on one of the other lectionary texts for the day. Some lectionary commentaries provide ideas for children's messages.

In some churches the children's sermon is not given by the minister but by members of the church staff or the congregation. There are both pros and cons to this practice. If the minister does not have this time with the children, the opportunity for the children to feel that the minister belongs to them is lost, as is the humanizing of the minister and the chance to hear the minister preach the Word on their level. It is also more difficult to coordinate the children's sermon with the rest of the liturgy if the same person is not preparing both.

There are positive aspects of including others, however: the opportunity to demonstrate the "priesthood of believers" by giving others leadership responsibility, the utilization of leaders who might be even more skilled than the minister in sharing the gospel with children, the opportunity for feelings of closeness to develop between the children and adult members of the staff or congregation, and a chance for the congregation to carry out some of its responsibility to nurture its young baptized members. Using lay leaders can also help give the leaders themselves a new understanding of worship as they try to correlate the message for children with other parts of the liturgy. However, even if others are invited to do the children's sermon on a regular basis, it still seems wise for the minister to do them often enough so that the "belongingness" mentioned in the first part of this chapter is established.

Ted Lazicki describes the ideal person to give the children's sermon: "Find one who, of course, loves and relates well to the children; one with a dramatic bent, who can tell the stories without embarrassment, using gestures, facial expressions, and at times, even costumes, that will delight and capture their minds and hearts."9

In *Bringing Up Children In The Christian Faith*, John Westerhoff lists five things we need to do to share our faith with children:10

1. Tell and retell the biblical story—the stories of the faith—together
2. Celebrate our faith and our lives
3. Pray together
4. Listen and talk to each other
5. Perform faithful acts of service and witness together

Although Westerhoff is addressing his words to parents, they are very appropriate for sermon-givers. It is easy to see how the first four can be accomplished through the children's sermon. The fifth is not as obvious, but we understand this time as a "faithful act of service" when we realize that the children are witnessing to the faith as well as being witnessed to.

A group of ministers were brainstorming the benefits of the children's sermon. They listed as positive attributes interaction with the children, helping children feel included, showing that the minister cares about them, providing a relaxed and comfortable moment in the liturgy, and providing an "affective" illustration of the sermon text. But the words that seemed to me to sum up everything that had been said were these: "It's a moment of grace."

A moment of grace. A priceless opportunity given by God to demonstrate love and care for our little ones in the same way that Jesus did when he said, "Let the children come"— this is the potential of the children's sermon.

FOUR

How Children Think

Children are not little adults. This should be obvious to all of us who have been exposed even to the dribbles of child psychology that come our way via TV sitcoms, glossy magazine articles, and problem-solving talk shows. But in reality we have not fully understood just what that "obvious" sentence means. We have not acknowledged that children think, reason, and feel in patterns that are unlike those of adults. Their psychological and emotional needs are different. Their language skills are not the same. If we are to share the "old, old story" with children effectively, we need to understand the basics of how they think and learn.

The scientific study of children's intellectual development is relatively new. It really began in the seventeenth century with the work of the Moravian bishop John Comenius, who held the "radical" view that education was to be related to everyday life and that girls were to be educated as well as boys. It was not, however, until the 1700s that Jean-Jacques Rousseau laid the foundation for what has come to be known as progressive (or child-centered) education. He observed children carefully, noted how they behaved and learned, and tried to adapt education to the child's level of development.

The churches, however, were slow to adopt these "new-fangled notions." The views of Rousseau and others were not popular with evangelical Protestants. The Calvinists railed against permissive child rearing and urged a sterner approach, not unlike that in Proverbs: "Do not withhold discipline from your children; if you beat them with the rod, they will not die. If you beat them with the rod, you will save their lives from Sheol" (Prov. 23:13–14, NRSV). Although children of Christian families were expected to be in church regularly, there was no religious education program designed with their needs in mind. Gradually, however, the change that was taking place in the secular educational system began to affect religious education as well. There was less emphasis on corporal punishment and more on the importance of love and gentleness. Church leaders and parents found that "beating them with the rod" was not the only way to save their children's lives.

After World War II, the study of child development received a tremendous boost from the work of the Swiss psychologist Jean Piaget. Piaget's impact on our understanding of how children grow and learn has been enormous. His work is cited in every major textbook in psychology, education, sociology, and psychiatry and has stimulated thousands of research projects. One leading developmentalist, David Elkind, goes so far as to say that "no contemporary social scientist can deem himself or herself fully educated without some exposure to Piaget."[1]

The study of children's thinking was Piaget's lifelong preoccupation. Establishing that human growth takes place in stages related to age, he focused on the development of reasoning in children and their construction of concepts such as objects, space, time, and causality.

Piaget believed that this development is orderly and that the stages are clearly defined. Although his description of these stages and their sequence has been generally accepted, it is important to remember that there is a wide variation in the ages at which these stages are reached. The ages suggested by Piaget are merely broad generalizations.

Piaget described the earliest stage, ages 2–7, as "preoperational," meaning that during this period children lack inductive and deductive logic. They do not understand cause and effect.

They put together unrelated thoughts, objects, and images without being aware of contradictions. For example, while adults might be amused at a shop window showing Santa and Rudolf at the manger scene, to a four-year-old this presents no problem. Preschoolers do not find the miracle stories in the Bible as amazing as adults do, because they do not see them as "irregularities."

Toward the end of the preoperational stage, children move into what Piaget describes as the "intuitive" phase, characterized by egocentrism, imitation, and the movement from learning through sensorimotor interactions to using intuition for understanding the relationships between things. It is important to remember that they are still unable to do abstract thinking. They need to have the great truths of the faith translated into terms they can understand, with illustrations out of their own experience. They will not be capable of abstract thought until about age twelve. Since the intuitive phase (ages 4–7) incorporates most of the audience for the children's sermon, we will take a closer look at some of the features of this period.

Understanding Concepts

The sermon-giver's task is to determine what young children can and cannot learn. One of the basic differences between children and adults is that adults identify concepts in terms of their properties or characteristics (a ball is something round that can roll); young children rely on examples (red ball). As early as age two they learn basic concepts, such as "dog," but not until age four or five do they begin to use broader concepts, such as "animal," or more specific concepts, such as "beagle." Donald Ratcliff suggests that the implication here is to make frequent use of "best examples" in teaching religious concepts to children, rather than attempting to teach concepts by stressing their abstract characteristics. For example, telling the story of the good Samaritan will teach children more about sharing than asking them to list three aspects of sharing. Practical examples of how they can share would help even more.[2]

One of Piaget's important discoveries about children is that they lack the ability to overcome the illusions presented by perception, "the way things seem to be." If a child is shown a tall slender glass and a short wide glass, each filled with the same amount of orange juice, and is asked, "Which glass has more juice in it?" the child will pick the taller glass. Likewise, it is hard for a child to believe the earth is not flat, because its roundness is not self-evident.

The orange juice experiment also reveals that young children have difficulty with what Piaget called "conservation." If juice is poured from the short wide glass into the tall slender one, children will say the tall one has more juice in it than the short one had. They are not able to "conserve" the first bit of information (the amount of juice) when the quantity appears to change simply by being in a taller glass.

This is the problem with most object lessons. The children are asked to "conserve" a piece of information about an object and transfer it to a moral lesson or a bit of theology. An example of this is an object lesson that uses a length of rope that the children hold for a short walk around the sanctuary. When they return to their starting point, the sermon-giver is to say: "Try to imagine a rope long enough for everyone in our church to hold. Everyone in our town. How about a very long rope, a rope long enough so that everybody in the world could walk together as we have walked today? Jesus' love is like that—a rope, a tie that binds all people together. Jesus' love helps people everywhere to walk together without getting lost, without stumbling. Just as our small group is joined together by this rope, so all Christians are joined together. We are all part of the one Christ Jesus, and we are all tied together by Jesus' love."[3]

This is a great analogy for older children and adults, but young children are unable to "conserve" the rope image and transfer it to Jesus' love.

Egocentrism

Piaget described young children as egocentric, meaning that they have great difficulty seeing things from the perspective of others. This is why it is difficult to teach a preschooler to share. According to Piaget, this is not the same thing as selfishness. Young children are not yet capable of seeing others as independent persons with their own feelings, wants, and experiences. As Lawrence Richards says, "Young children do not apply the Golden Rule simply because they cannot!"[4] Not only are they not in tune with the needs and wants of others, but their failure to share is also a reflection of their belief that their toys and treasured possessions are part of themselves and sharing them is like sharing an arm or a leg. My four-year-old granddaughter, Maggie, does not want to be separated from her blankie at night, and losing Pink Bunny was a near catastrophe! They "belong" to her in a more intimate way than just being possessions; they are part of her. This does not mean we should not continue to try to teach unselfish love, but we must be prepared for some degree of failure in the very early years. This kind of insight will help us evaluate young children's behavior more objectively.

Equilibration

Another important term in Piaget's developmental theory is "equilibration." This is exactly what it sounds like: achieving balance and harmony. As children develop, they struggle to make sense of the realities they encounter, which are not always what they seem. As understanding grows, harmony is achieved, until some new reality comes along that has to be struggled with, and the imbalance starts all over and new cognitive growth is required to reach equilibrium again. In other words, when things in the child's picture of the world no longer fit, the child has to work hard to reorder his or her universe. Children are always unlearning and relearning as well as acquiring new knowledge. They are not blank slates; they acquire knowledge through their interaction with the environment, but as these interactions take on new dimensions, their knowledge stretches and changes. This constant reshaping and adjusting cannot be forced. Piaget believed that children are eager to know and that a primary part of the educator's task is not to dull this enthusiasm for learning but rather to stimulate it by asking questions, by "wondering" with the children, and by encouraging new learning through helping them question and investigate. This should be an important part of the children's sermon.

Time Perception

Another key difference in adults and children is time perception. Most of us are familiar with the difficulty in explaining to a three-year-old how long it is until Christmas, or a birthday, or a planned vacation. In a TV interview, Arthur Ashe, the celebrated tennis champion, spoke about the difficulty of communicating to his five-year-old daughter, Camera, the effect that his AIDS might have on their future together.

> Time means nothing to her. I say to her, "I'll take you to Disney World next month."
> "When is that?"
> "In 30 days."
> "How long is that?"
> For Camera, the future is tomorrow afternoon.

The crucial thing to remember is that young children are just beginning to understand time duration. They have a very limited sense of chronology, of past and future. We must not expect them to have a very clear sense of biblical history—or of their own history, for that matter. It is not uncommon for a four-year-old to say, as my granddaughter did, "We already have our Christmas tree; we got it tomorrow."

Memory Retention

Children's memory depends not only on the stage of their mental development but on other factors as well. They remember better if they have seen as well as heard. They remember what is said better if it is presented clearly and simply, rather than in a disconnected, rambling style. If children are to remember children's sermons, the sermons must be carefully prepared and well organized. We also need to bear in mind that what children remember about the sermon over a period of time may not resemble the original experience very closely.

The use of "memory work" has been controversial in religious education, but it is an important part of the learning process. When children demand to hear a favorite story over and over again, it is because this is one way for them to learn: by remembering. Constant repetition is not boring or monotonous to preschoolers; it is an essential ingredient in the learning process. However, we must recognize that even when children can successfully quote Bible verses or sing songs from memory, we cannot assume that real learning has taken place. Rote learning does not necessarily produce growth in understanding or increase the child's ability to make sense out of the world. The danger is that rote learning will be substituted for real comprehension.

Memorizing short verses or liturgical responses can be an effective part of the children's sermon. However, if memory work is used, care should be taken not to give young children tasks beyond their abilities. They should be presented with a limited amount of material to learn, and it should be given in small doses. It is easier for them to learn a verse two or three words at a time. Children are easily frustrated when expected to learn too much. The content should also be appropriate for their level of understanding.

A reminder: Piaget taught that, for the child, doing is a requirement for learning. This means that instead of just stressing the memorization of words and facts, we should use teaching strategies with children that involve seeing, touching, and imitating.

Religious Understanding

Although Piaget wrote nothing about the religious education of children, his work has provided the foundation for the work of theologians and religious educators seeking to know how to share the faith with children. Lawrence Richards is one who believes that Piaget helps us recognize that just as the child's view of the world changes as he or she develops mentally, so the child's religious understanding is also modified with cognitive and conceptual development. Concepts of God, of Jesus, of prayer, of death and resurrection, of Christian spirituality grow and change as the child grows and changes. Richards writes:

> What is important is that children *have* faith concepts that they can use at every stage of development to guide them in their exercise of faith responses in life. It is our task in ministry with children to teach them what they need to know, in ways they can understand and experience, and guide them lovingly to live out that simple faith that Jesus chose to commend.[5]

Piaget's work helps us understand that we must use a situational approach in sharing the faith with children. Instead of teaching broad, abstract concepts, we bring biblical truths into the child's world to interpret specific situations or events. Piaget's understanding of equilibration shows us that it is as children interact with their environment in various situations that they develop their understanding of what is happening. We need to teach the truths of the faith that will help them make sense of their day-to-day life experiences.

A child's response to the faith story is fresh and intuitive, not the result of logical thought. One problem with Piaget is that despite his tremendous insight and wisdom about children, he puts his emphasis on the development of logic and reason. We must be careful not to dismiss the intuitive insights of children and to recognize that the Holy Spirit works in their lives as well as in the lives of adults. It would be well for us to remember that, like the wind, the Holy Spirit most often works in playful, unpredictable ways that defy logic and reason (see John 3:8).

I sat next to a young couple and their two-and-a-half-year-old daughter at a communion service. Communion was being served by intinction (dipping the bread in the cup), and as the family returned to their seats after being served, I heard the little girl whisper to her mother with a radiant, confiding smile, "I thought about Jesus." Of course, she may have just been saying what she thought her mother expected of her, but I prefer to think that the winds of the Spirit were blowing as she intuited the presence of Christ and, in her simple childlike way, made her response of faith.

For the Master said, "Truly I tell you, whoever does not receive the kingdom of God as a little child will never enter it" (Mark 10:15, NRSV).

FIVE

How Children Grow in Faith

In the last chapter, we reviewed Jean Piaget's contributions to understanding the development of the child's intellect and logical reasoning powers. Other scholars have thought about development from the standpoint of personality development, social development, moral development, and faith development. In this chapter we will take a brief look at these forms of development and consider their implications for sharing the faith with children.

Personality Development

Any discussion of developmental theory would be incomplete without a consideration of the work of psychoanalyst Erik Erikson. Erikson developed a schema of eight stages to describe how individuals work through various life crises at certain chronological periods. One of his primary contributions to the study of child development was in the exploration of the tasks that belong to each age if healthy personality development is to occur. He also stressed the importance of relationships with "significant others" that enable or inhibit healthy growth. Erikson described each stage in terms of the basic tension that must be resolved during the period. For the purposes of this study, we will examine only the first four stages.

Stage One: Trust vs. Mistrust (birth to age 1)

In this stage, the child's personality development depends on the quality of the relationship with the primary nurturer, usually the mother. If the child feels accepted, he or she learns how to be accepting of others.

The role of the faith community is important in helping establish a place that is in itself trustworthy and testifies to the trustworthiness of God. Urban Holmes suggests that what children learn during the first year of life influences the kind of religious faith that will be possible for the rest of their lives.[1]

Stage Two: Autonomy vs. Shame and Doubt (1–2 years)

By stage two, the child has found a voice and learned to say no. He or she is beginning to accommodate the self to society and the environment. The temptation of parents and teachers is to overcontrol, but that can threaten the growth of positive self-identity. Both firmness and tolerance are needed. The child is discovering the meaning of freedom, with its risks.

Stage Three: Initiative vs. Guilt (3–6 years)

The task of this stage is to develop initiative, but there is a crisis when activities are initiated that incur adult disapproval. If adults restrict the child's behavior too much and are over-controlling, the result may be a sense of guilt that will hold the child back from achieving his or her full potential in life.

It is important in this stage for the sermon-giver to accept the children's curiosity and not put down their need to know and to question. This can help their sense of initiative out-weigh their sense of guilt. Children need a lot of affection at this stage, but adults must realize that these same children may have ambivalent feelings toward them, because of this conflict between initiative and control.

Stage Four: Industry vs. Inferiority (6–12 years)

Here we find rapid development of the skills necessary for adult functioning. There is a strong desire to work and to achieve. The problem is that children begin to evaluate themselves against others in terms of competency in schoolwork, popularity, and even athletic prowess. If they see themselves as incompetent, the result may be a lasting sense of inferiority and a low sense of self-worth that may last through adulthood. It is important for the sermon-giver to remember that children's play is their work and to provide ways to stimulate their minds, curiosities and imaginations.

In evaluating Erikson's work, it is wise to keep in mind Lucie Barber's discerning words:

> When I speak of levels of development . . . I do not intend that you think of pigeonholes. I am certainly not suggesting that children can be classified as belonging in this or that box. Development, as far as is known, is not so simple as climbing from Step 1 to Step 2 and forever hereafter Step 1 is done. The psychologists Erikson and Maslow suggest to me a sponge model. Persons can develop up through levels, but can always partially drop behind to a former level depending upon the holes in their personal sponges.[2]

Social Learning Theory

Another important implication for children's faith development is provided by the social learning theorists. Their emphasis is on the assumption that behavior is learned and that personality is shaped by interaction with others: family, friends, teachers, and role models.

This is a significant theory for the community of faith, for it stresses the power of close, loving, supportive relationships and of good role models. The following five important concepts are associated with social learning theory.

Socialization

Socialization is the process of interaction with others by which a child becomes a responsible member of society. Through socialization, children develop language and relational skills, judgment, and self-control. It is the process by which they learn about the traditions and values of their own culture.

The persons who have the greatest impact in early childhood are those in the child's immediate family, especially parents. Through discipline and role modeling, parents help shape the child's growing personality. Studies have indicated, however, that it is the quality and not the quantity of this parental care that determines healthy development.

As children grow older, their horizons of social awareness expand to include schoolmates, playmates, other significant adults, and the faith community. The impact of all these increases as the child begins to look outside the home for role models and new ideas of behavior and values.

The children's sermon can play an important role in socialization, not only by providing interaction with others but by being an instrument for the transmission of the tradition and values of the faith community.

A good illustration of how this is done is provided by John Hinant's children's sermon, "How Big Is Your Family?" After a discussion of different kinds of families, Hinant goes on to describe the church as a family:

> The family of God is the church. Yes, you are part of that family. You belong in church, where all of us are like brothers and sisters. Some of us are like big brothers and big sisters, who are to make a place for you and care for you in this wonderful family God has given us that we call "the church." God wants this special family to show the world how much God loves us and how loving we can be. We are to make room for the stranger and the visitor within our special family

until there is no one who doesn't share the kind of love we know in our families. When this happens, everyone will feel like brothers and sisters, with Jesus as a kind and helping big brother and God as a parent who will always love us.[3]

This message uses concepts and images that will be familiar to the children as it affirms the role of the community of faith in the child's socialization process.

Role-modeling

Socialization takes place primarily through observation and imitation of the behavior of social models. Children are not born with a concept of right and wrong and what constitutes permissible behavior, but as they incorporate the values of their parents or of other significant adults, they develop a conscience.[4]

What makes a child choose a particular person as a role model? Lawrence Richards suggests four factors, all of which are important considerations for the children's sermon-giver:[5]

1. A long-term close relationship marked by warmth and affection
2. Opportunities to observe the model in a variety of life situations
3. Having the model explain his or her behavior
4. Having the model reveal the beliefs, values, and feelings associated with that behavior

Notice that it is important for the role model's values to be explicitly stated and explained, as well as lived out, so that the growing child makes connections between the model's observed behavior and stated beliefs.

A moving example of how this was done by one pastor was recounted by David Steele, pastor of Christ in Terra Linda Church in San Rafael, California. Steele had suffered the loss of his closest friend on Friday, and when the time came for the children's sermon two days later, he suddenly broke into uncontrollable tears of grief.

> So there I was, sitting with the children in worship, and those tears of mourning for pal Bill were flowing down my cheeks and I couldn't regain or pretend control. I had to acknowledge my tears before those children. I did not do so very eloquently. I told them simply about my friend and about the many happy times we shared. I told them that while I knew Bill was with God, I was sad about his leaving. That I missed him and kind of hurt inside. They could tell I was sad. They were right, but I wouldn't stay sad. They'd see me laughing again before long.[6]

What a marvelous example of role-modeling, not only for the children but for the adults in the congregation as well!

Role-taking

Role-taking is the ability to see things from the perspective of other persons. It is not quite the same as empathy, because even when young children understand another's viewpoint, they often seem to lack the capacity to care. Once again, their egocentrism gets in the way. Role-taking is important because of its link to moral development. Children's moral decision-making is influenced by their ability to understand another's viewpoint. Using storytelling as a sermon method is an effective way to help young children understand and respond feelingly to the perspective of another.

Identification, Imitation, and Internalization

This is the process of responding to the attitudes and behavior of another by adopting them as one's own. Observation of a model leads to trying to imitate the model's behavior. The crucial element, however, is internalization. It is not enough to simply mimic another. True learning takes place when the imitated action becomes a part of the child's pattern of behavior. A two-year-old child can learn to parrot "thank you" in response to parental urging, but when the child internalizes these words as an indication of true gratitude and appreciation, another stage in learning has taken place.

Reinforcement

Social learning theory recognizes the importance of the reactions of others to a child's behavior. When the reaction is positive, the child receives positive reinforcement in terms of praise or reward. If, however, the reaction of others is negative, the child receives negative reinforcement in the form of scorn, ridicule, punishment, rejection, or sometimes simply a lack of response. The children's sermon provides a good place for positive reinforcement as the sermon-giver receives the children's comments and questions with words of approval and encouragement.

Moral Development Theory

Lawrence Kohlberg related Piaget's theory of stage development to moral thinking. He was convinced that the way persons make moral decisions is related to their stage of intellectual development. He also included dimensions of social learning theory by acknowledging that moral thought is influenced by parents, peers, role models, and all kinds of personal interactions.

Kohlberg described three levels of moral development, each of which has two stages. For our study, the significant level is Level One, the preconventional level.

Kohlberg believed that children up to age nine seldom pass this level. This means that young children do not make their moral decisions on the basis of society's rules or because of the "universal-ethical principles" (as Kohlberg phrased it) that govern the upper levels, but out of deference to authority figures who have the power either to reward or to punish.

Stage One: Punishment-and-obedience orientation. At this stage the physical consequences of an action determine its goodness or badness. This stage is governed by carrot-and-stick morality: If you do something wrong, you'll be punished; if you do right, you'll be rewarded. Kohlberg feels that most young children, because of their egocentrism, operate at this level. Parents frequently find they get a better response by using a Stage One approach with very young children than by trying to use the reasoning methods of the other levels.

Stage Two: Instrumental-relativist orientation. Right action is that which satisfies one's own needs and occasionally the needs of others. This is the marketplace mentality. It's summed up in the phrase, "You scratch my back and I'll scratch yours." Equal sharing and fairness can be understood, but primarily because one's own needs are being met. Doing good to others is not yet a matter of justice or loyalty or altruism.

Kohlberg reminds us that children's moral reasoning is not the same as that of adults. We cannot expect them to "do what is right" on the basis of reasoning that makes sense to us. We cannot teach abstract moral concepts and expect children to apply them to their lives in the same way adults would. Instead, we would do best to give them concrete examples of "honesty" or "forgiveness" in the form of actions they can imitate, until they begin to appropriate this form of behavior automatically.

Faith Development Theory

In recent years, scholars have sought to pull together the varied developmental threads into a single tapestry in order to understand more clearly the intricacies of how faith development takes place.

Among the first to explore this issue seriously was Ronald Goldman. His work showed that mental ability and age were major factors associated with the development of religious thinking. He created new styles of curriculum materials, based on age-level-appropriate theological concepts. Although criticized for its liberal theological perspective, Goldman's work has been widely accepted and remains influential.

In the early 1960s, David Elkind began doing serious study in the cognitive development of religious understanding. His work reinforced the findings of Goldman, as he discovered a uniformity in children's ideas at certain ages that gave way in later years to conformity with adult perceptions. He maintained that

> while adults believe children and adolescents are most like them in their thoughts and least like them in their feelings, it is the reverse which is true. Before eleven or twelve most children were not able to understand religious concepts as they were understood by adults, but instead they gave meanings to them which reflected their own views of the world.[7]

It was the work of James Fowler, however, that brought faith development theory into its own. Fowler took the work of Piaget, Kohlberg, Erikson, and others and constructed a six-stage outline of how faith develops. He related conceptual and intellectual development to religious norms appropriate to the various stages. Fowler's process of synthesizing the findings of the various schools of developmental theory has made it possible for educators to take seriously the developmental approach in the preparation of curriculum materials for different age groups.

Fowler called the period up to age three "undifferentiated faith," a time when the basic attitudes of trust, courage, hope, and love are formed in young children by their relationships with significant adults. He followed this with these six stages:

1. Intuitive-projective faith (ages 3–6)
2. Mythic-literal faith (ages 7–11)

3. Synthetic-conventional faith (ages 12–17)
4. Individuative-reflective faith (ages 18–30)
5. Conjunctive faith (30–40)
6. Universalizing faith (after 40)

For our purposes, we will examine closely only stages one and two.

Stage One: Intuitive-Projective Faith

Fowler agreed with Piaget that children in this stage are incapable of abstract thought, that cause and effect are not clearly understood, and that it is difficult for them to separate fact from fantasy. Their imaginations take over to close the gap. Fowler gives the example of a six-year-old's response to the question, Can you tell me what God looks like? His answer: "He has a light shirt on, he has brown hair, he has brown eyelashes." Fowler notes the difficulty in parent-child dialogue at this stage when the child's logic in asking questions works in quite different ways from the parental logic producing the answers. As Piaget established, children during this period are very limited in their ability to see things from another's perspective, since they assume that their own perspective is the only one there is. Because of their egocentrism, their conversations with other children of this age are what Fowler calls "dual monologues, each speaking in a way that assumes identity of interest, experience, and perception, while neither coordinates his or her perspective with that of the other." This is the source of many of the flare-ups of temper that characterize this age. Fowler accepts Kohlberg's understanding that moral decision-making, at this stage, is based on reward or punishment, not on abstract notions of what is "just" or "right." Social awareness extends to the family and a few significant others. Authority resides in parents and significant adults. The children also respect the authority represented by uniforms and roles. They see life in terms of separate episodes without a sense of chronology or relatedness.

If a child this age recounts a movie plot, the result is a listing of episodes in the movie that were vivid to the child, without showing how they were connected. For this age there is a solid link between symbols and their reality. Santa isn't just a symbol of parental love; Santa is Santa.

Children in this stage combine fragments of stories and images from their faith traditions in their own way to talk about God and sacred things. The result is sometimes a curious blend of fact and fantasy. Even children from nonreligious homes do not reach school age without an image or images of God.

Fowler agrees with Bruno Bettelheim, who insists it is a mistake to present children at this stage only with the sunny or cheerful side of life. Our tendency is to want to protect them from life's grim realities, but even very young children worry about death. Biblical stories can be effective ways to help children deal with their anxieties and fears by providing models of courage and conviction in ways that "prove life-opening and sustaining of love, faith, and courage." Fowler says that education at this age "has a tremendous responsibility for the quality of images and stories we provide as gifts and guides for our children's fertile imaginations."[8]

Stage Two: Mythic-Literal Faith

While stage one was characterized by the blending of fact and fantasy, children in stage two become serious about separating the two. They want to know what is "real." They investigate and test ideas and want "proof." This was illustrated by an episode of the television series *I'll Fly Away* in which seven-year-old John Morgan agonized over the reality of Santa Claus. "It's really you, isn't it, Dad?" he asked worriedly. John Morgan is afraid of what the truth might be but feels impelled to ask anyway.

One of the key developments of this stage is narration. Children make sense out of the world by telling stories about it. It is a prime time for sharing the great stories of the Old and New Testament and for helping children develop their own gifts of storytelling. These stories are crucial in helping them sort out the experiences of their lives. As Fowler says, for them "meaning is trapped in the narrative."

At this stage children are beginning to understand cause and effect and want to investigate why things are the way they are. In spite of this, their thinking is still concrete and literal. They are not yet ready for the abstract thinking of adulthood.

They have a limited but growing ability to take the perspective of another. Their understanding of God is anthropomorphic, but since they are beginning to be able to take another's perspective, they can differentiate God's perspective from their own, as in ten-year-old Millie's answer to the question, Does God care when you do something wrong?

"Sure he—he cares. And he knows that you're—he knows that you are sorry about it. And he always tries—he always forgives you, usually."

Children at this age take the religious concepts they have learned at home and at church and filter them through their own perspective. Both their moral and faith understandings come from the reciprocity principle, the "you scratch my back; I'll scratch yours" idea. This affects their understanding of God as well. God will reward those who are good or who "do things" for God. The limitations of this stage, the literalism and the emphasis on reciprocity, can result in perfectionism and "works righteousness."[9]

Summary of Implications

Taking into consideration the findings of the developmentalists, let us now attempt to construct a profile of the children to whom we address our children's sermons. How do they think and feel? What are their limits and their capabilities? What are the most important things to remember as we try to share the faith with them?

Ages Two to Six

We have seen much evidence in developmental studies to support the idea that the early years of childhood are crucial in providing the foundations of later adult faith. Sophia Fahs has found as a result of her study of the experiences of children that "small children have emotional experiences that are the seeds of religious sentiment; and that the natural way of spiritual guidance would begin with these experiences and let the larger understandings grow slowly as the experiences increased."[10] If she is correct, it is crucially important for us to have a clear picture of what happens in these early years. By distilling the findings of the developmentalists, we find significant attributes of the early years that may provide the "seeds of religious sentiment" of which Fahs speaks.

They are egocentric. Preschool children operate in terms of their own interests. The ability to cooperate and join in group activities develops gradually. Although by age four they are beginning to develop some empathy toward others, it is very rudimentary and they still have great difficulty in being able to imagine what others might be thinking or feeling. Sermon-givers should be aware of this and not assume that preschoolers are able to empathize as adults do.

They are unable to think abstractly. This is a factor to consider in telling stories. Young children may overlook subtle abstract points and focus only on the obvious ones. What they remember may not be the "significant" theological point the storyteller was trying to make. Children's sermons should be as concrete as possible.

They are confused by symbolism. Sermon-givers should be careful about the use of religious language and metaphor. When children hear "the church is God's house," it may be a very confusing image for their literal minds. The next chapter will examine the use of symbolism in more detail.

They are curious. Preschool children have been described as "walking question marks." Arnold Gesell and his associates reported that children's questions usually come in this order: where, what, why, who, and how, representing a deeper and deeper plumbing on the part of the child to find a kind of wholeness of meaning.[11] Sermon-givers should recognize that children's questions are legitimate requests for knowledge and take advantage of the opportunity to expand their world by building in new experience.

They live in a world of imagination and fantasy. Young children are not surprised by miracles. Everything for them is, in differing degrees, miraculous, since the laws governing physical regularities are not clearly understood. Awe and wonder are more natural to them than to jaded "you-gotta-show-me" adults.

Concepts are best taught by example. Children's grasp of concepts is based on their experience with concrete examples. They learn abstract concepts such as forgiveness and unselfishness best through specific illustrations and stories that model them.

They have a limited understanding of personality. The preschool child sees personality in terms of good or bad. It is hard for them to understand that persons can be mixtures of both. This suggests the sermon-giver may need to delete some facts or simplify Bible stories, so only the dominant traits are stressed.

They crave acceptance and affection. Most child psychologists agree that, to obtain a desired response, positive comments are better than shaming the child. The sermon-giver needs to be sensitive to when a child needs the comfort of a pat or an encircling arm and when a smile from afar is all a child is ready to accept.

Ages Six to Eight

Their horizons are expanding. There is less emotional dependence on the dominant caregiver and more of a sense of belonging to groups outside the home. The sermon-giver can encourage this sense of belonging by providing an atmosphere of warmth and acceptance. Not only are the relationships of six- to eight-year-olds expanding, but they are gaining new experiences through television, reading, movies, and school, that can be referred to in children's sermons.

Their reasoning ability is developing. Piaget described this age in terms of the ability to do "concrete operational thinking," meaning the children are now capable of understanding cause and effect and can figure out how to do things. They are beginning to be capable of some limited abstract thought. Fantasy continues to be important at this age, and children still have the desire to attribute magical properties and explanations to marvelous events.

They still have a limited concept of time. Even eight-year-olds are not able to grasp the span of biblical history as time. "Long ago" to them is last week. It is better for sermon-givers to focus on people and events rather than facts of chronology.

They are assimilating and accommodating information. New knowledge is incorporated by internalizing and using it. Children are able to modify their thought processes to incorporate new learning. Their sermon provides a wonderful opportunity to add to knowledge about the faith and help children assimilate this knowledge into their own life experiences.

As we look back on these early years of childhood, it helps us not only to understand what is happening in the lives of the children with whom we are working, it also helps us understand our own faith journey in a new way. As one person said, "I feel more and more how essential to any wider development and spiritual growth the early understanding of my own faith was, and is. It was the point of departure and, like all points of departure, still needs, for me anyhow, to be visited and relived from time to time. The road winds back but the road is not the same."[12]

SIX

The Spiritual Needs of Children

Ruth Robinson, wife of the Bishop of Woolwich, John A. T. Robinson, states a vital issue for children's sermons:

> It is the particular problem of our generation of parents and children to know how to share with our children the depth and dimension of Christian experience in terms which do not distort it. But they themselves provide the clues if we will listen. As children they need help in "working it out themselves," below the conscious level, in their relationships with those they trust, so that later on they may have the content of experience with which they may "fill out the words" and the tradition they have inherited.[1]

How *do* we share the faith with children "in terms which do not distort it"? The developmentalists have given us some clues to help us build those relationships of trust in which children "experience" the faith. The issue we must now explore is how to go about helping the children "work it out themselves" and what the content of their faith experience should be.

In 1939 a teacher in New Zealand, Sylvia Ashton-Warner, developed a remarkable teaching style for her work with young Maori children. Later she wrote a description of her methods in a book titled *Teacher.* She spoke of her role in these terms: "From the teacher's end it boils down to whether or not she is a good conversationalist; whether or not she has the gift or the wisdom to listen to another; the ability to draw out and preserve that other's line of thought."[2] If we are to be effective in our efforts to share the faith with children, we must learn to be good conversationalists, which in Ashton-Warner's experience meant being good listeners. She writes that the best student assistants she had were "modest and self-effacing," while the worst was "a very clever girl who was an insatiable talker and who talked everyone else to pieces on the subject of herself."

Being good conversationalists with children begins with recognizing that, as the developmentalists have shown us, children are not little adults. It means taking into consideration the discoveries that have been made about how children learn and recognizing the implications of those discoveries for the growth of their spirituality. In *Bringing Up Children in the Christian Faith*, John Westerhoff says that children possess naturally the essential elements for having faith. The kingdom of God is first perceived in the world children know best. He describes this world as one of feelings and intuition, of dreams and visions, of not fretting about the past or fearing the future, of learning from experience, of finding miracles believable, of sensing the presence of God, of being able to live simultaneously in seen and unseen worlds.[3] In *Will Our Children Have Faith?* he goes on to suggest that faith develops like the rings of a tree, each of which increases the complexity of the tree but does not change its basic nature. The earlier rings are not lost but added to. Just as a tree does not grow in a vacuum but needs a good environment, so faith grows in response to our experiences in the world.[4] Westerhoff describes the growth of faith in three stages: affiliative faith, searching faith, and mature faith. Affiliative faith is the period of childhood, in which the foundations of faith are laid through direct experience: through imitating others and through learning to trust others, ourselves, and our world. He believes that the gift of faith is directly related to a family's participation in the community's rituals, symbols, and myths and that belonging to a community is very important in order to fulfill our need to be wanted and accepted.[5]

What are the spiritual needs of the children to whom the children's sermon is addressed? What experiences can we provide that will help the tree rings develop? Recognizing that faith is a gift, what can we do to facilitate the reception of that gift? In this chapter, we will look at the spiritual needs of various ages as they have been discerned by religious educators and child development specialists.

Ages Two and Three

Spiritual Needs

Although in larger churches toddlers are not usually included with the children who are gathered together for the children's sermon, the reverse is true in smaller church settings. Toddlers frequently accompany their older brothers and sisters to the front of the church. The minister is not always filled with delight, because their presence increases the difficulty in attracting and maintaining attention. What are the special needs of this age group?

They need *acceptance* by adults who will stimulate their development by their loving presence. Grace is communicated through relationships. Adults need to be constant and steady, patient and tender, but firm.

They need *respect for their autonomy.* The development of independence is the major developmental task of this age. They need a balance between order and disorder, firmness and flexibility. Love balanced with consistent discipline lays the foundation for a healthy self-concept and an ability to be intimate with others and with God.

They need *religious ritual.* They need to hear stories about Jesus and his love for them. Judith Allen Shelly says, "Religious beliefs and customs, when practiced regularly in an atmosphere of love, are also extremely important to toddlers and preschoolers. Mealtime grace, bedtime prayers and Bible stories, and going to Sunday school and church can be deeply meaningful and comforting."[6] John Westerhoff believes that ritual must always be at the heart of Christian education and says emphatically, "If our children are to have faith, they must worship with us."[7]

Theological Understanding

It is difficult to know exactly what very young children think and feel about the theological concepts adults take for granted. Theology is an abstract discipline, so it is extremely hard to interview preschoolers who have not developed the ability to think abstractly. They understand and feel more than they can express. Nevertheless, through observation and paying sensitive attention, those who work with the religious education of children have established the following assumptions about children's theological capability and needs. They are not "scientific," however, in the stricter sense of sociological research.

God. God is generally perceived by two- and three-year-olds as one who gives us the world, family, friends, and daily food; one who is good, loving, and trustworthy; one who understands our hurts, fears, and angers; one who is near in darkness as well as through the day. Little children need to be encouraged to find God in the concrete wonders around them (water, butterflies, sunshine, springtime). They need to be helped to develop a sense of awe and wonder toward the Creator of all the good things in their world. We do this largely by our own excitement, by our own sense of awe and wonder. "Children always learn more by what we do than by what we say, and if our reaction to the sunset, the flower, or the spider's web is mediocre, they are able to sense that lack of excitement."[8]

Jesus. Small children need positive attitudes about Jesus as a guide and friend. They are not yet able to understand his role as redeemer and savior. It is better to talk in human terms about Jesus, to tell stories of his goodness and kindness, and to use him as a role model who shows children how to be good and kind too. Make the connection between "baby Jesus" and the grown man who loved and helped people, so that children understand they are the same person.

The Bible. Even young children can understand that the Bible is a special book which tells us stories about God and Jesus. The stories used should be very simple, joyous, and happy to help alleviate the fears and frustrations of this age. Good illustrations are important. Flannelgraph pictures are excellent at this age so that children can feel as well as hear and see, since this is what Piaget described as the sensorimotor stage. They should have simple Bible storybooks of their own.

Prayer. Even two-year-olds are capable of saying grace or prayers. For most, it is an expression of thanks for good things in their lives. At age three, they begin to understand that prayer is talking to God. Prayer continues to be primarily an expression of gratitude. It should begin with adoration and move to thanksgiving. Lucie Barber suggests that too often we have tended to start children with petitionary prayers. "Let Santa Claus receive petitions," she says. That prevents children from seeing God as mean or stingy when their requests are not answered.[9]

Ages Four and Five

Spiritual Needs

Studies of children in this age group indicate that they understand religious concepts when stories have action and interesting characters. They are capable of finding meaning for their own lives in the stories. They can parrot back information, but often what we assume are their ideas are only verbalisms, words used superficially in the right context but without any real understanding. An example of this is the way they reply with the words "God" or "Jesus" to almost any question asked of them during the children's sermon. One story goes that the sermon-giver, in a nature-oriented sermon, asked the children, "Who has a bushy tail and swings from limb to limb in the trees?" The prompt response from one child was "God."

The problem is that these children are still in the period of concrete, literal thinking; since most religious words are abstract, they are at a loss. Teaching the chronological and historical facts about religion must be accompanied by a more subjective or intuitive approach, using poetry, music, art, drama, and dance, in order to help them experience the awe and wonder that accompany the mystery of the faith. Their spiritual needs have increased.

They need to feel loved and accepted by the church, to have *a sense of belonging* to the family of faith.

They need *"attitude education"*: to be helped to grow in faith, hope, and love as children of God.

They need to develop *moral values* by being encouraged to find alternative ways of acting when their tendency is toward selfish behavior.

They need *to explore relationships* through interaction in play and conversation. Good relationships with significant adults lay the foundation for a good relationship with God.

They need *to be loved and to be loving.* They can accept the idea of grace toward themselves but have difficulty with extending grace toward others. The idea of justice, in an adult sense, is beyond them.

They need *stability and security.* When they can trust others, they feel safe and can relax. They need to understand that God is one on whom they can always rely. Sermon-givers can help relieve the anxiety of these children by being confident, warm, outgoing, and trustworthy.

They need *adult role models* who can show that they are human. If adult leaders are relaxed, children will be more at ease.

They need *an assurance of God's presence* to alleviate their fears. They need to be aware of God's love and care for them. Using Bible verses such as "Do not fear" or "I will not be afraid" can help them develop confidence in God's protection.

Theological Understanding

God. Belgian researchers studying Catholic children discovered that their understanding of God fell into three stages. In the first stage (up to age 3) God is seen as "object" and later, as children develop in their understanding, as "human." God "lives" in the church, and children are curious about his physical activities. "What does God wear?" "Where does God sleep?" Sometimes the priest is mistaken for God.

By age three or four, God is seen as superhuman. At this age the child wants to see God and is frustrated when told that God is in heaven or is invisible. The child wants to know how far heaven is and how to get there. Later, God is understood to bring all that is needed as well as things the child requests in prayers. At this point, the child's religion seems to be completely selfish; God is there simply to serve the child. God is recognized as being more powerful than mere human beings.

The third stage (from 4 1/2 to 6) identifies God as "divinity." The child understands God to be both beyond space and time and immanent. God is recognized as maintaining the order of nature and also supervising family life, being the parents' partner and the child's friend as well as a model. The child assigns God the possibility of knowing everything and granting every wish. As one child expressed it, "God is the chief of everything." God is seen as powerful, both watching over people and punishing their wrongdoing. Children this age show a real interest in knowing God and pleasing God.[10]

A considerable amount of research indicates that young children's images of God stem from their perceptions of their parents—both what they actually are and what the child thinks they should be. Iris Cully elaborates. "Like a parent—

mother or father—God fed his people, guided them, corrected them, forgave them, and never forsook them. Human fathers are not perfect, but the child can find security in the assurance that the divine parent is always dependable."[11]

A 1986 study showed that children this age often associate God with fun and play, seeing God as "a permissive deity who was concerned with children's welfare and who performed certain functions for them."[12]

At this age, God is still anthropomorphic, but young children have a readiness to understand God on many levels, as the Belgian study just cited shows. Even though most children believe God lives in a definite though faraway place called heaven, they can also accept that God can be both far away and close at hand.

As God becomes more familiar, preschoolers have a generally positive attitude toward God, which increases their trusting attitude and their feeling of safety.

Jesus. There is often confusion between God and Jesus. Jesus is frequently seen as having superhuman powers, just as God does. Jesus is also seen as a "model child," someone to try to imitate. Most children with a religious upbringing identify Jesus as someone loving and concerned to help them. Many pray to Jesus as well as to God, depending on how they were taught. Jesus is generally understood to be a human person, but there is often no connection in their minds between the infant Jesus in the manger and the grown man. Jesus is often thought of as a friend and companion.

Prayer. David Elkind's studies of prayer and children ages five to seven indicate that prayer is understood "only vaguely as a verbal activity about God, rabbits, dogs, fairies, deer, Santa Claus, Jesus, Mary, and Mary's little baby." Children at this age are primarily concerned with getting something they want through prayer. They associate prayer with certain fixed times—going to bed, before eating, or going to church. Unanswered prayer distresses them more than it does older children.[13] Lucie Barber feels that a big mistake is made by educators who teach young children to ask in prayer for God's comfort and strength. She asserts that God's comfort and strength are adult concepts, and the connection to God is much too abstract for children. As an example of a dangerous petitionary prayer, she mentions "If I should die before I wake." She says, "These kinds of prayers also run the risk of placing God again at a disadvantage in children's eyes. When these prayers are unanswered, God is less than a success to children. The fears remain; God has failed. I do not think it is necessary to run this risk."[14] Barber feels that at best prayer for small children is "talking to an important, magical 'somebody.'"

Other research indicates that boys and girls are different at this age. Boys tend to pray more irregularly and less frequently. Girls are more likely to say they have experienced God's answers to prayers.[15]

Prayer is primarily taught by the example of parents and teachers. Grace at meals and bedtime prayers are important teaching opportunities. So are spontaneous moments of adoration and appreciation for sunsets, mountains, moonlight. At these times "children receive the stimulus of parents' awe, adoration and thankfulness."[16] If prayer is a part of the children's sermon, it should be done with deep feeling instead of being just a perfunctory way to dismiss the children.

Ages Six to Eight

Spiritual Needs

During the early school years, children are still more at home with religious emotion than with religious thought. It is important, however, for them to be exposed to religious experiences and ritual even before they understand their meaning. Their understanding will grow as their reasoning ability develops. As Iris Cully puts it, "Children apprehend more than they comprehend."[17] They learn from ritual and from the worshiping community, as well as from religious activities in the home. At this age they have a literal view of justice, so it is important not to expect an adult understanding. They are beginning to have more empathy for others and to understand that God cares for others, even those different from themselves. They have particular spiritual needs.

They need *to be a part of a worshiping community:* to participate in rituals and the celebration of religious holidays with their families.

They need to develop *an understanding of God* as one who is always dependable and trustworthy, even when parents are not. This assurance of God's care is important to their sense of self-worth.

They need to have *a sense of wonder* about Jesus and a recognition that he was different. This lays the foundation for their confession that Jesus is, indeed, Lord.

They need to be aware of *the different ways God is known:* as Creator to whom they can turn in every need; as Jesus, loving, healing, and reconciling; and as Spirit, making it possible for everyone to grow in love.

They need *help in deciding what is right* in certain situations, rather than being given absolutes.

They need to see religion as a way *to experience forgiveness,* learning how to be forgiving and understanding the meaning of reconciliation.

Their need for *a sense of accomplishment* should be taken seriously, and they need to be helped to learn the biblical tradition and its application to everyday life.

Theological Understanding

God. For the most part, God is viewed anthropomorphically in concrete human categories and is seen primarily as providing for physical needs. Research indicates that "relatively few children at any age really understand the terms traditionally used to describe God in worship or in the catechism."[18] However, they are capable of reverence and awe at the thought of God and are just beginning to grasp the more abstract concepts of God as spirit or love, not confined to one place. By age eight or nine, children begin to understand God as all-knowing and all-powerful but also as loving parent.[19] God is generally thought to be in heaven or in the sky and is generally understood as creator, protector, and moral judge, much like their parents.

Some studies indicate that boys and girls have different religious ideas. Boys have a more socialized religion, identified with relationships mediated by ritual activity, and girls a more loosely structured religion with a close personal relationship with God.

Jesus. Jesus is understood both as God and as a living historical person. There is confusion in children's minds about how Jesus lives both on earth and in heaven. They are familiar with stories of Jesus' birth, death, healing, and raising the dead. They are ready now to understand the conflict in Jesus' life: his criticism of the religious leaders and their opposition to him. It is possible to arouse a sense of awe and wonder about Jesus: his birth, the adoration of the crowds, his resurrection. This awe can be the beginning of a confessional attitude as they recognize the uniqueness of Jesus and can proclaim, "Jesus is Lord."

Prayer. At this age, prayer is still viewed in terms of requests for particular activities or things, but there is the beginning of a shift to thanking God for things already received and a concern with more altruistic requests. In other words, prayer is becoming more personal and individualized but less egoistic and self-centered.

A Final Word

Stan and Jan Berenstain are known not only for their bear stories for children but also as practical philosophers of family life. In their humorous little book *How to Teach Your Children*

About God . . . Without Actually Scaring Them Out of Their Wits, they write about parental dilemmas in talking about faith issues.

Most parents manage to steer a middle course between the remote God of the universe and that fearsome fellow who is so ready your soul to take if you should die before you wake, and find a good way to tell Junior about God in terms he can understand and relate to.

The Berenstains then illustrate this point with a cartoon that contains the following dialogue:[20]

FATHER TO SON: . . . The rain, the sunshine, the rainbow—they're all God's work, son—all part of God's Great Plan.

SON: You mean God made everything—everything in the whole wide world?

FATHER: That's right, son!

SON: Did he make trees?

FATHER: Of course!

SON: And flowers?

FATHER: Absolutely!

SON: And butterflies?

FATHER: Everything!

SON: Did he make spiders? belly aches? measles? pollution? earthquakes? tornadoes? floods? wars?

At this point, the father gives up and "socks the kid into Sunday school so fast his head spins."

The reality is that not even in Sunday school, or in the children's sermons, will all the questions be answered. Thank goodness, this is not our task. Our task is to be good conversationalists, to provide a relationship of trust in which searching questions can be asked. Our responsibility is to share with children the biblical stories that will help them respond to God in love and grow in their understanding of the faith. Above all, as sermon-givers we are to be ready and willing to reveal our own emotions of awe and wonder in the light of our love for God, our commitment to Jesus Christ, and our enthusiasm for the church as the body of Christ.

SEVEN

Language and Symbolism

"When I was a child, I spoke like a child, I thought like a child, I reasoned like a child; when I became an adult, I put an end to childish ways" (1 Cor. 13:11, NRSV).

With these words, Paul put his finger on one of the most common failings of children's sermons: as adults we no longer speak as children do. We have "put an end to childish ways" and in the process raised a barrier to effective communication.

Jerry Jordan, author of several books on children's sermons, writes, "Words not only have a *say* but also a *sway* in our lives, all of which requires us to note carefully the effects our words may have on others."[1]

How do we talk to children? What effect are our words having on the lives of those little ones who face us Sunday after Sunday? Are there guidelines for the use of metaphor and symbolism? How do we know when we are communicating well and when our words fall on deaf ears?

Many problems with children's sermons have to do with the use of language. Words are used that are out of the range of children's comprehension; abstractions are piled on top of abstractions until the "fog index" is so dense even the adults listening from the congregation are lost. Storytelling is not done effectively and loses the attention of the children. Most complex of all, perhaps, is the questionable use of metaphor, idiomatic speech, parable, and symbolism. Adults frequently make the mistake of assuming that children's comprehension is like their own. As we have already seen in our survey of developmental theory, nothing is further from the truth. It is possible to use all these forms of speech with children, but some guidelines are needed.

The communication problem is further complicated by the fact that much of our theological language is itself abstract and therefore communicates little to children. It takes great care and thought to be able to share the language of faith without using too many abstractions. Terms that seem basic and familiar to adults through long usage—terms such as grace, justice, righteousness, salvation, wholeness, redemption—are in themselves abstractions and may have little or no meaning to children if not set in concrete contexts. As James Carr warns, "There is nothing wrong with introducing children to the language of faith, but when too many words are included which children cannot understand immediately, the possibility is lost for reaching their thoughts as well as their affections."[2]

In spite of this caveat, it is important that children learn to use the significant terms of the faith. There are some things we can do to help them. We can define terms as we use them, we can give concrete examples of what the terms mean, and we can relate them to the experience of the children. All it takes is practice and a willingness to think patiently about our use of theological terms and the assumptions we make about children's understanding of them.

Communication

Since language is basically communication, one of the important aspects of growing language development is the child's ability to use it to communicate with others. The child learns quickly to use words, not only to convey ideas and meaning but also to establish who he or she is. Connections are made between individuals through speech. We reach out to others as we talk and listen. We express our needs and hopes and become aware of the needs and hopes of others in our dialogue together. Our words become instruments of trust and love or tools of animosity and distrust.

Skills must be developed to enable a child to hear another's point of view. These skills are called "referential communication skills." Piaget discovered that very young children have limited referential skills. Their conversation often simply accompanies action instead of being a real attempt at communication. In other words, they speak "at" rather than "to" one another. Good communication means openness, give-and-take, being willing to listen as well as talk. Children must learn how to do this as they move from the early stages of egocentrism into real empathy and dialogue with others. It is a process of growth.

Language Use at Different Ages

Ages Four to Six

Communication is very limited during this period. As we have seen, children talk mostly to themselves even when in groups. Piaget called this "egocentric speech" or "collective monologue" and found it existed more between peers than toward adults. It is fascinating to watch two four-year-olds playing together. Each one carries on a running commentary on the action in which he or she is engaged, but except for occasional directives given to the other, what occurs can hardly be called a conversation. Their egocentrism keeps them preoccupied with what they are thinking, and they have very little empathy for the concerns of the other child. It is because of this that a child will frequently interrupt children's sermons to launch into a narrative about whatever particular concern is occupying his or her mind at the moment.

Children's silliness and expansiveness carry over into their language; they like playing with words and making up funny new words and sounds. They love exaggerations and words like "enormous," "gigantic," and "colossal." They like onomatopoeic words as in "The boat went 'splish, splash' in the water." They like repetition: "Step, step, step went the donkey carrying Mary."

This is the age of the Why? question. Don't hesitate to say "I don't know" or "Let's find out." Because of the egocentrism of this age, these kinds of questions are best answered in terms that relate directly to the child. It is important to hear what they are really asking, to treat their questions with respect and not cut them off with exasperation and annoyance.

Not all Why? questions are alike. Some are simply asking for reassurance that things are really as the child sees them. In answer to "Why does the sun come up in the morning?" an answer that makes sense to the child is "To keep us warm." There's no need to explain the entire planetary system.

Other Why? questions might have psychological implications. ("Why does Daddy have to go away?") These questions are sometimes simply expressions of a need for reassurance. Still others demand concrete reasons or rules for the way things are. ("Why does the choir sit at the front of the church?") None of these Why? questions need long philosophical or scientific answers in the early years, but they do deserve our patient consideration.

Ages Six and Seven

By age six, children are learning how to use speech for communication and this becomes an important socializing factor. They are beginning to be able to carry on conversations in which they are really listening and responding to others.

We take for granted that children know how to use connecting words that link one thought to another. However, because cause and effect is still only dimly understood at age six, certain words are used in very limited ways. "Because" is one of these, and "although" is another. They are more likely to use sequential words, such as "then," which link ideas but do not explain them in terms of cause and effect.

The Use of Metaphor with Children

Metaphor is the primary way in which we speak about God. Therefore, the ability to use and comprehend metaphors seems essential to any religious understanding. Psychologists have had a strong interest in metaphor and have discovered that nothing about it is as simple as it appears. Educators and biblical scholars have shown a similar interest in understanding the use of narrative and story. The increased attention to these literary forms has raised questions about how children understand metaphor, idiom, and parable.

A 1928 study of how children understand metaphor showed that children's comprehension of metaphorical material was unrelated to their attendance at church or other religious involvement but directly related to their mental development. Other research has shown that the type of metaphor makes a big difference and that context is of prime importance, as children's experience with the context is almost essential to their understanding of the metaphor. Although young children may be able to parrot simple metaphorical speech, they have difficulty understanding satire, analogy, metaphor, and irony, all of which require advanced language abilities. Yet how often these are used by well-meaning adults trying to interpret the faith to children! We are so accustomed to addressing adults with these forms of communication that we fail to remember they are lost on children. It is astonishing how many of the Saturday morning cartoons on television are loaded with these very elements of satire, analogy, metaphor, and irony. Little children seem to be engrossed, but in reality they fail to understand these expressions in the way adults do. They are literalistic in their thinking, and metaphorical imagery confuses them. Object lessons are most often visual metaphors, and one of the chief problems with their use is that children do not easily make the transference from the object to a faith lesson for their own lives. Object lessons are actually much more appropriate for youth and adults.

If metaphors are to be used, here are some suggested guidelines.

Choose the metaphor carefully. Adults may understand what it means to "sow the seeds of the Word," but such an abstraction is beyond the reasoning abilities of children.

Use metaphors that come from a context familiar to the children. Most experts feel that it is difficult for children to see themselves as "lost sheep" in the parable and to tell four- to six-year-olds that they are to be "ambassadors for Christ" is to use a metaphor outside their experience and understanding.

If you do want to use a metaphor such as "ambassador," it should be prefaced with an explanation or a story that illustrates its meaning. The metaphor then becomes a simile, as children are encouraged to see how they can be "like" ambassadors by telling others of God's love.

Using Parables with Children

Parables are extended metaphors. A popular definition of a biblical parable is "an earthly story with a heavenly meaning." Although parables seem at first glance to be wonderful material to use with children, because of their story format, the problem is that children do not readily make the transfer to the "heavenly meaning." Adults have reached a stage of cognitive development when they are generally able to hear parables on several levels and understand their deeper meanings. We must bear in mind, however, that Mark records that Jesus' disciples did not always understand his parables (Mark 4:13).

Sallie McFague, who has written extensively about the use of parables in theology, says that parables, through the use of imagistic language, put "familiar things in an unfamiliar context" and give us new insights for our lives.[3] We enter into the parable, and life and faith are reinterpreted for us by that experience. It's not hard for children to understand the story of a parable. Understanding its hidden implications presents the difficulty. Even children ages ten to twelve think in such a way that it is almost impossible for them to interpret and explain the meaning of a parable, unless it is accompanied by a specific illustration from everyday life that relates to their own experience. For instance, the meaning of the parable of the lost sheep could be understood if it were connected to the experience of being ostracized, excluded, or lost. This still does not mean that children will understand the full meaning of the parable as it was originally intended.

The lost-sheep parable has been the subject of some intensive research. It was found that children under the age of five who heard this parable concentrated on its concrete actions and objects (the sheep, the shepherd, the fold, the shepherd's crook). They loved the story but did not see themselves as sheep. Between ages five and eight, children began to understand simple analogies (comparing the lost sheep to a child being lost). It was not, however, until the high school years that a truly reflective attitude toward the parable led to a deeper understanding of it.[4] It seems evident to most researchers that very young children understand parables best when they can relate to one of the characters. Jerome Berryman uses parables in his teaching but insists that children become familiar with the story by playing with materials related to the story so as to gain some experience of their underlying metaphors. Berryman has collaborated with Sonja Stewart to produce a book that outlines this method of teaching the parables. In the preface to *Young Children and Worship*, he says:

> My focus is on the function of religious language— parable, sacred story, and liturgical action—in the moral and spiritual development of children. I am especially interested in how this powerful language discloses a

"world" where God is present to help cope with and transcend the existential issues—death, aloneness, the threat of freedom, the need for meaning—that box us in and define children and adults as human beings.[5]

Fowler's faith development theory gives some support for this position for children ages six to twelve. Since these children use narrative to make sense of their worlds, Fowler feels there is no need to add a moral or a point to stories. If the child is immersed in the story, it speaks to him or her with its intrinsic richness. Excellent examples of stories that do this are the children's stories of C. S. Lewis and Katherine Paterson.

Using Symbolism with Children

All human beings have their own particular sets of symbols. Even young children use symbols, but they do not always use them in the same fashion as adults. The Christian faith is rich in symbols; in fact, symbolic action and ritual may be far more powerful than intellectual knowledge about the faith.

Because they are affective rather than cognitive, symbols speak on many levels. They express our deepest desires, our yearnings, our feelings. They give wings to our aspirations. However, like metaphors, in order for them to be meaningful to children they must be associated with concrete, meaningful experiences. They should be instruments of awe and wonder, as they point to ultimate spiritual meaning. They should stimulate both thought and feeling; they should enrich and beautify children's lives.

It is our task to prepare the way for this by helping the child relate the symbols of the faith to meanings they will later claim more fully, both intellectually and emotionally.

Many symbols can be introduced and explained in children's sermons. They include the cross, candles, the lamb, the good shepherd, the fish, the vine and branches, the Bible, and the liturgical colors. Agnes Peery shows how to give good, simple explanations of Hebrew symbols such as the mezuzah and phylacteries.[6] Symbolic acts that can be included as part of the children's sermon time are bowing heads, folding hands, and kneeling. Symbols in the sanctuary can be pointed out and explained, such as the communion table, candles, the baptismal font. It may be possible to see some symbols in the church's stained glass windows or in architectural carvings. In the second chapter, on worship, we mentioned having children present for baptisms and the Lord's Supper, two of the great symbolic acts of the faith.

We must always remember that children will not think about these symbols in the same way adults do. They will not understand fully and completely what the symbols of the faith mean, but it is evident that these symbols can exert an important hold on their feelings and make lasting impressions on their minds. The ornaments on a Chrismon tree representing the Trinity or Christ the Ruler may not be explainable to a young child, but the impact of their beauty and richness can create a mood of reverent awe in even the youngest child.

Iris Cully says, "When in doubt, keep away from the symbolic." However, if you must use symbols, use them like this: The rainbow reminds us of God's promise to take care of everyone; the cross reminds us that Jesus loved people so much he died for them.[7]

EIGHT

The Shape of the Sermon

Now that we've thought about the worship setting, looked at the psychological development of children, examined their spiritual needs, and surveyed the problem of language and symbolism, we arrive at a crucial question: What methods are most effective for the children's sermon?

There are several schools of thought about the form children's sermons ought to take. There are those who favor the object lesson, those who like to use casual dialogue or questions and answers, those who prefer storytelling, and the ambitious souls who revel in elaborate dramatizations. Perhaps most sermon-givers prefer a mixture of styles, varying the method with the sermon's intent.

How Children Learn

The starting place for determining appropriate methods of teaching in any situation is the basic question, How do people learn? or, more specifically for our purposes, How do children learn? As we saw in chapters 4 and 5, the developmentalists have given us many clues. It is our task to apply these clues specifically to the preparation of children's sermons.

Jerome Bruner has described four elements in a child's

learning process: curiosity, the drive to achieve competency, the process of identification, and reciprocity.[1] How does each one of these inform our preparation of the children's sermon?

Curiosity

The child wants to know how, what, and why. One of our tasks is to create an anticipatory atmosphere so that curiosity will be aroused. Jerry Jordan, author of *Filling Up the Brown Bag*, always uses a prop that is hidden away in a paper bag. After he has built up suspense about what is in the bag, he reveals it. One of the problems with this approach is that the children's attention is riveted on the object, which may distract them from the message.

There are other ways, however, of setting up situations in which curiosity will be aroused. Good storytelling can create a mood of anticipation. Appropriate questions can stimulate imagination, if they are questions of genuine interest to the children and not too abstract or vague.

The Drive to Achieve Competency

Iris Cully has come to the frightening conclusion that our Christian Education programs have not really encouraged children to deepen their understandings of God, of Jesus, of the Bible, or of prayer and worship.[2] If Christian Education programs and classes have failed to develop competency, how can we expect our five-minute children's sermons to do it? Perhaps we need to consider seriously making biblical storytelling a top priority for this time.

Identification

Whether we are comfortable with it or not, the truth is we become role models for children when we sit down with them for the children's sermon. If we are lukewarm about what we are saying, if we are simply mouthing platitudes, the children will be lukewarm too. Our attitude toward the Bible and toward prayer will be revealed by our tone of voice and gestures as much as by what we say. Do we consider the closing prayer merely a way to wind things up and send them back to their seats? It will be evident. Do we approach the children's sermon with dragging feet and fuzzy preparation? They will know.

On the other hand, if we truly enjoy children, if we look forward to those few minutes together, they will know that too. If we are to communicate anything meaningful about God's love and care, we must demonstrate that love and care in our own lives. Neutrality doesn't work; enthusiasm does. Religious understanding is acquired only where religion is practiced and not just spoken about.

Reciprocity or Cooperation

As we approach the children's sermon we should remember what it felt like to be a small child. This remembering should be the first step in our preparation. What did it feel like to be in the presence of your pastor? Were you shy? Were you afraid or awed? Did you always want the closest seat, or were you the one on the outer fringes? Use these memories to help you understand the situation of the children.

Reciprocity also means helping the children enter into the stories, to experience the gospel story as their story. When we tell the story of Jesus welcoming the children, each child listening should feel welcomed by Jesus also. Experiencing the gospel story means making a response to it—not just an intellectual response but a response expressed in our daily lives and choices. When children are able to make this kind of response, they have really learned the Bible stories.

The Teacher's Role

Not enough can be said about the importance of the teacher's role. Paul said to Timothy, in an effort to strengthen his faith, "You know who your teachers were" (2 Tim. 3:14, TEV). Paul was reminding Timothy of the models of belief he had known and how they had laid a good foundation for Timothy's faith by the testimony of their lives.

Perhaps no attribute is more essential for the teacher of young children than flexibility. This can be defined in many ways: being willing to adapt your agenda to the situation at hand, handling with ease the unexpected question or response, having a sense of humor, taking questions seriously, being willing to admit you don't have all the answers, being patient when things don't go as planned, and affirming insights and contributions offered by the children. It is so easy to make children feel that their ideas or contributions are ridiculous or wrong by a flippant response or an ill-timed laugh. Put-downs have no place in the children's sermon.

One of the chief hazards of children's sermons are surprises: the unexpected answer to innocuous questions ("Where did you get your name, John?" "From Jesus"), the personal family revelations ("My mother and daddy had a fight last night"), the wanderer who disappears behind the pulpit, the interjections about recent vivid experiences (trick-or-treating, a new puppy, a sore finger) which may not connect at all with the story you are trying to tell. A sensitive teacher will not surrender to anxiety or ill temper but will maintain an easy, confident manner and a positive approach. Trust yourself, trust the children, but don't let the situation get out of hand. Be tolerant about interruptions but resist the temptation to play to the adult audience by making asides to them ("Well, I got more than I bargained for!").

Affirmation is a key ingredient of the teacher's role. Rejoice in the children and the ideas and insights they express. It's all right to help a child complete a phrase or sentence, but don't take over the contribution. Receive it as valuable. If it seems to be irrelevant, thank the child and move on or, if possible, rephrase it so it fits with the topic. Think of children's speech as poetry. It is not so much rational and logical as it is full of butterfly glimpses of their reality. Try to catch the glimmer before it flies away.

Approaches to Children's Sermons

The Object Lesson

The use of visual objects is a favorite approach. The way in which objects are used varies widely. Some favor secrecy. The object is hidden in a bag or behind the pulpit, to be displayed only after curiosity has been aroused. Others favor a more impromptu format, asking the children to bring objects and selecting one to be the focus of an on-the-spot children's sermon. Frankly, I feel this impromptu approach violates all the principles for good children's sermons: it is not related to the adult sermon and it demands no previous thought or preparation; it is an opportunity for the sermon-giver to show off and seldom produces an atmosphere of awe or wonder. In short, it is a gimmick, used primarily by those who are unwilling to put time and thought into careful preparation.

There are two basic problems with object lessons. First, they fail to take seriously what we have discovered about how children think and learn. As we saw in chapter 4, young children do not have the capacity for abstract thought and therefore are unable to make comparisons between objects and religious truth. They cannot "conserve" the object and relate it to the religious truth you want to teach. While they may enjoy drawing butterflies at Easter, it is confusing to them to relate the butterfly to the resurrection. When object lessons are primarily exercises in symbolism, the point is generally lost on children. The use of a bird's nest or an autumn leaf, on the other hand, may be an effective teaching tool, as a reminder of the wonderful things God has made but not because it represents an abstract concept such as forgiveness, freedom, or salvation. Anytime we find ourselves using the words "like," "stands for," "because," or "since," we need to be on guard, for these are expressions involving abstractions. Children relate things to one another, not to abstract ideas.

The second problem is that the object becomes the central focus and can even divert children's attention from the main point of the sermon. Children want to play with the object, particularly if they have been invited to touch or hold it, and then lose interest in the idea we are trying to convey. Later, they may remember the object but not the explanation.

Defenders of the object lesson claim they are using good pedagogical principles: visual aids enhance learning. They also claim that when children can remember the object, they can also remember the point of the sermon. Object lessons are valued as attention-getters, especially useful when there is a wide age span. However, as Eldon Weisheit cautions, "It is better not to get the attention of the hearers at all than to get it and lose it. If you never get their attention, they may not notice that you had nothing to say . . . but if you have their attention and then have nothing to give them, the lack of a clear point will be obvious."[3]

If we do decide to use an object as part of our presentation, here are some good principles to follow.

Choose an object that will help children understand the point of the sermon.

Choose one that is simple, easily understood, and for the most part familiar to children's experience.

Objects can be effective as props for stories. Even unfamiliar objects may be used if they are related to the story. To illustrate biblical stories you might use a shofar, a menorah, a shepherd's staff, yeast, pottery, or a scroll.

Using objects from nature can help children feel wonder at God's goodness and appreciation for the beauty around us and can help them express thanks to God for the goodness of creation. These might include autumn leaves, flowers, bird's nests, or seeds to plant.

Take-home objects can help children remember what was said: palm branches on Palm Sunday, fish shapes, simple crèches at Christmas.

Other objects that can be very effective are pictures, art prints, musical instruments, puppets, and felt board. These are often used to illustrate a story or a particular point and, when used properly, can be powerful instruments of awe and wonder.

The Discussion Format

Using a discussion format is both appealing and tricky. It is appealing because it establishes an informal, cordial atmosphere of give-and-take. The children's input is sought and their contributions welcomed. It is tricky because of the unpredictable nature of "child-speak." A child's honesty can be refreshing or embarrassing. Some seasoned veterans avoid this approach because of the difficulty of handling off-the-wall comments and questions.

Presbyterian minister Ginny Ellis has compiled a list of helpful suggestions. "Listen to their comments or objections; their point may be better than yours! Their sharing is a gift to you and to the church; treat it with respect." She also cautions about listening too long to each child and suggests reestablishing control without putting the child down by using phrases such as "I want to hear more about that later" or "We're about out of time; let me finish up, OK?" or even "Someone else needs a turn to talk now." Ginny reminds sermon-givers to repeat the children's main points for adults in the congregation who can't hear the whole conversation. This is important to keep the whole worship service inclusive.[4]

It is important to use good questions to invite discussion. The Sunday before Election Day, a minister asked a group of young children, "What are we going to do this week?" The question was lost on them; voting was simply not a part of their agenda. Ask questions that capture the children's interest, such as "What would you do if . . . ?" or "Have you ever seen a . . . ?" Keep them open-ended if possible, trying not to ask questions that have only one right answer, or those that can be answered with yes or no. Don't ask, "How many disciples did Jesus have?" but, rather, "How do you think Peter felt when Jesus called him to leave his boat and follow him?"

Questions about feeling allow us to enter into the story more fully than questions about fact.

Asking the right kind of questions takes great sensitivity to children's interests and understandings. The best way to learn how is through experience and practice. Talk to young children as you visit in their homes. Engage them in conversation in supermarkets and on playgrounds. Visit young children's classes and take notes on the kinds of questions experienced teachers ask. Good children's sermons are not born in a vacuum. If all your contacts during the week are with adults, the shift into "child-speak" is very difficult.

What about wrong answers? We itch to correct them, set them straight, and sometimes we do it in a way that shames and embarrasses. If a wrong answer is given, give the correct answer, but do it in an encouraging and kind way.

Right answers deserve positive reinforcement: praise, approval, hugs, encouragement, and above all our attention. Phrases such as "That's right!" or "What a good answer!" assure them their contributions are worthwhile. When a child responds to a question with "I don't know," try to give some encouraging hints, such as "Could it be . . . ?"

If we choose the discussion format, it is extremely important to hone our listening skills. The greatest affirmation we can give children is our listening; it shows we take them seriously.

Using Special Occasions

Special moments in the life of the church provide wonderful opportunities for children's sermons. Two of these occasions are baptism and the Lord's Supper. Children are more likely to be present for the former than for the latter, but they should have the opportunity to participate in both.

Baptism. Baptism is a profoundly moving time in the life of a congregation. It is a symbol of belonging and a deeply moving experience for the entire congregation. Children are no exception. They respond to it with fascination.

In many services, baptisms are held early enough in the

worship service to take the place of the children's sermon. Children are generally invited to sit on the floor or in the front row, so they can see exactly what is taking place. By using simple, clear language, the minister can explain to the children that baptism simply means becoming a part of the church family, a family of people who care about one another and help one another, even tiny babies. In one congregation, a charge is given not only to the adult members of the congregation but to the children themselves: "Will you help her, teach her, and play with her?"

Agnes Junkin Peery gives an excellent example of how to teach about baptism in her book *Let All the People* in the sermon "Thinking About Infant Baptism." This sermon is not designed for a baptism Sunday but invites the children to look into the baptismal font and remember how the water in it is used. The discussion then moves to the specialness of baptism, the promises that are made, and how baptism says that we are a part of the family of God. She suggests that the children and the congregation chant (or sing) together the words of Richard Avery and Donald Marsh's song "We Are the Church" to reinforce this concept of belonging.[5]

The Lord's Supper. While the language of the Lord's Supper is difficult for children to understand, an insight into its meaning can be given by relating it to other celebrations that include special meals, such as Christmas, Thanksgiving, and birthdays. The Supper can be talked about in terms of Jesus' sharing of a special meal with his friends and how he wanted his friends to share meals together to remember him. Simple explanations are best; too much theological explanation is confusing.

The Experiential Model

Educators long ago discovered that the best way to teach is to involve students in experiential learning. While we remember only 10 percent of what we hear, we remember 90 percent of what we experience.

Brant Baker has described a way of doing children's sermons based on the concept of learning by doing in his book *Let the Children Come*. Baker's approach is based on the understanding that children learn best by experiences that include the affective dimensions of learning as well as the cognitive. In other words, the gospel becomes real for them when they incarnate it. He describes the process for developing his sermons in four steps:[6]

1. Definition of the general topic, text, theme, or idea to be communicated, usually at least two days in advance
2. Dreaming the question: If we could do anything to experience this topic or text, *anything*, what would we do?
3. Assessment of resources on hand: usually people, objects, and places
4. Modification of the dream to reality

Obviously, this approach cannot be undertaken on the spur of the moment. Baker makes it clear that careful preparation is necessary. He often involves the entire congregation in the storytelling and warns that it may take a few months before the congregation realizes that it is expected to participate. While some of his examples are a bit flippant (Christmas Story falls short on the mystery he claims to be seeking to convey), others are excellent. I found the reenactment of Paul and Silas in prison particularly well done. It makes the story vivid and points to the wonder of God's power. In it, he asks the children to sit in the middle of the church in the aisle. Volunteers are asked to be Paul, Silas, and the jailer. The members of the congregation seated in the ends of the rows near the children are asked to stand and join hands to form a "prison wall." The story is then told very simply by the sermon-giver. Paul and Silas are asked to sing "Jesus Loves Me." The "walls" (congregation members who are standing) shake, and so do the children. The sermon-giver feeds lines of dialogue to Paul and the jailer expressing the jailer's dismay,

Paul's reassurance, and the jailer's subsequent confession of faith. After a few summary words, the sermon-giver ends with a prayer of thanks to God for the faith of Paul and Silas and for the mighty power of God.[7] This simple reenactment, without props or costumes, will make the story come alive for the children and for the congregation as well.

The strength of the incarnational approach is in its linking theology to action and in the power of participatory action to help children experience and remember the faith tradition. Its weakness is that children may get so caught up in the doing they will not hear the gospel message. (Shouting "Hey, Joe!" during the Christmas storytelling may prevent them from feeling wonder at the Christmas mystery.)

Even without going to the elaborate minidramas that Baker proposes, there are other ways to involve children experientially. Here are some basic guidelines.

Ask questions relating to experiences the children may have had, such as "Have you ever been afraid?" "Have you ever argued with someone?" "What do you like best about summer?" Don't expect "right" answers, but really listen to what they have to say about their experiences.

Make use of the five senses. Children can "participate" in the biblical story of creation by touching leaves and seeds and smelling flowers or by acting out how animals move and birds fly. If you are telling the story of David and the sheep, help them enter into the story by having a piece of wool to touch.

Encourage the children to make various liturgical responses to prayers, such as "We thank you, God" or "God's name be praised." Here is an example of a simple litany based on Psalm 139 that could be a part of a children's sermon:

ONE PERSON: When I am awake,

EVERYONE: God is always with me.

ONE PERSON: When I am asleep,

EVERYONE: God is always with me.

ONE PERSON: When I am talking,

EVERYONE: God is always with me.

ONE PERSON: When I am hiding,

EVERYONE: God is always with me.

ONE PERSON: When I am very small,

EVERYONE: God is always with me.

ONE PERSON: When I am growing up,

EVERYONE: God is always with me.

ONE PERSON: When I am afraid,

EVERYONE: God is always with me.

ONE PERSON: When I am thinking,

EVERYONE: God is always with me.

ONE PERSON: When I don't understand things,

EVERYONE: God is always with me.
Thank you, God, for being with me.[8]

An unusual children's sermon would be to have the children lead the congregation in the Lord's Prayer with hand and body motions. They will need to learn the movements ahead of time. See *Including Children in Worship* by Elizabeth J. Sandell for diagrams of this and other worship responses.[9]

Do walk-arounds. For example, take the children to look at the baptismal font, a stained-glass window, the communion table.

Let the children interact with the congregation. Let the children take to members of the congregation something they have previously made for them, such as a bookmark or a heart printed with the words *God loves you.*

Find ways for children to participate in special times. In the paragraph on special occasions, we have seen how children can take part in a baptism by responding to questions asking them to take responsibility for the baptized infant. Children can also participate in other special occasions, such as lighting the candles on the advent wreath, joining a Palm Sunday procession with palm branches, or adding flowers to an Easter cross.

Story

There are few children who do not respond positively to the magic words, "Let me tell you a story." I am convinced that storytelling, and preferably biblical storytelling, is by far the best method for the children's sermon. There are many reasons for this conviction. Stories are more than just entertainment; they enable children to hear the truth on a level that makes sense to them. Abstract ideas take on concrete form and definition through the experiences and behavior of the characters in the stories. Love, kindness, forgiveness, and obedience are given flesh and blood through well-chosen stories with which children can identify.

Biblical Storytelling. In 1972 Johanna Klink wrote, "Christian faith can live only in a larger community than the family, in which the faith is celebrated together and the old story continues to be told century after century."[10]

If Klink is right, the most essential stories for children to hear are the ones from scripture. I am constantly amazed at how few children's sermons tell that "old, old story." Although there is a place for stories based on contemporary experiences, I agree with John Westerhoff, who has said, in reference to sharing our faith with children, that we need to "tell and retell the biblical story—the stories of the faith—together." Speaking to a group of educators, Walter Brueggemann said, in similar fashion, that the most important responsibility we have to children is to tell them the biblical stories, over and over again, so they come to know them even before they understand them. There is a wonderful description of the power of biblical storytelling in Naomi Ragen's novel *Jephte's Daughter*, as Batsheva, a young Jewish woman, reflects on her childhood.

Some of her earliest and happiest memories involved Sabbath afternoons. Sitting in her father's lap, the back of her head pressed into his shoulder, she never tired of listening to his patient retelling of the stories of the Torah, which were as beloved and familiar to her, as firmly entrenched in the life of her imagination, as Cinderella, Snow White, and The Three Pigs were for other children. Rachel and Leah, Sarah and Abraham, were as close and real to her as her parents, her friends.

Her favorite story was "Akedat Yitzchak," the near sacrifice of Isaac. The shivers would run down her spine imagining kind old Abraham, who had waited so long for a child, holding his cherished son's hand and leading him away to be sacrificed because God had asked him to. She imagined the old man's terrible sadness and fear and yet his brave steps forward. She imagined the boy's trusting eyes fixed upon his father, his faith never wavering even as he laid himself flat upon the rock and waited. And because she knew it would all end well because God was good and hated cruelty of any kind, and that father and child would get all the credit without actually sacrificing anything, the story always made her happy.

She loved those instances in the Bible where people took flying leaps of faith headlong into the fearsome unknown and God was always there, like a good father, His arms outstretched to catch them: the children of Israel plunging headfirst into the swollen waters of the Red Sea; Daniel in the lion's den; Moses defying Pharaoh. Not only did they all come through unscathed, but they were also showered with rewards. All you had to do was believe.

And as she listened to her father, trusting implicitly in every word he said with every ounce of her mind and heart, she sometimes forgot that these were God's words and not her father's, imagining that he and God were one, teaching her how to be wise and good, directing her steps and keeping her from all harm.[11]

What Ragen is describing is the power of story to place children in the situations of biblical characters and allow them to "shiver" with them, experience trust through them, and be reassured of the guidance and loving care of God by them. Ragen makes it clear that these stories have a powerful ability to convey a sense of wonder.

The importance of biblical stories does not lie primarily in their cognitive aspects, in the factual information they convey, but in their affective side. They have the power to speak personally to children, and they demand a response. They teach us "how to be wise and good," as Ragen says.

When selecting a biblical story to use, an obvious place to start is with the scripture passage that will be the text for the sermon later in the service. It is not necessary to use the entire text or treat it in the way the adult sermon will. You might select one paragraph, or one sentence, or even one word from the text upon which to build the sermon. Another suggestion is to use a secondary text to which there might be a reference in the body of the adult sermon. Either of these methods allow you to coordinate the children's sermon with the rest of the liturgy. By relating the scripture to the children's experience, you have an opportunity to express the gospel message in terms children can understand. (See Carolyn Brown's *Forbid Them Not* series for ideas.)

If the text chosen for the adult sermon is not appropriate for children, you might try one of the other lectionary passages for the day. When none of these texts seem adaptable to their

needs, choose one of the many Old and New Testament stories that children can understand. A good resource for learning
to tell stories with rhythmic cadence and simple words is
found in the *Read-Aloud Bible Stories* series by Ella K. Lindvall.
These books are captivating retellings of scripture stories. Each
one ends with a "What did you learn?" summary such as this:

> What did you learn?
> Jesus was pleased
> when the man
> thanked him,
> Jesus is pleased
> when *you* tell Him
> "Thank you."
> What could you
> thank Jesus for
> right now?[12]

These summaries provide an excellent way to open dialogue about the story.

When using biblical material, here are a dozen guidelines
to remember.

Be faithful to the text. Don't twist its meaning to make it
say what you want it to say. The point of the story of Jesus
cursing the fig tree (Mark 11:12–14) is not that "sometimes it's
all right to be mad."

Remember the purpose: not to teach Bible trivia but, as
Jerry Jordan says, "to draw attention to the person of Jesus,
the presence of God and to how those in the Bible have believed."[13]

Use your creative imagination. As you work with the text,
try to see it through the eyes of a child.

Avoid miracle stories. Young children need to think of
Jesus not as a magic worker but as someone real, who loved
his friends and helped people in everyday ways and who
loves and cares about us.

Remember your time limitations and condense your story so you don't have to hurry through at the end. Five or six minutes is not a very long time. Practice ahead to get your timing right.

Don't hesitate to *be dramatic* with voice and gestures. A good storyteller gets into it!

Use repetition and action words: "The honk-honk of cars, the zoom-zoom of jets, the beep-beep of buses, the drip-drip of water, the splish-splash of puddles."[14]

Keep your main idea in mind. Focus! Limit the story to a single episode, with a minimum of characters.

Simplify your vocabulary. Use terms children know or explain unfamiliar ones.

Make stories personal.

Use pictures, flannel boards, or puppets to make the stories more visual. Make sure they are large enough for all to see.

Finally, and most important, "*Approach the text in holy innocence,* asking: What is God saying to us in this lesson?"[15]

Stories from Everyday Life. The Bible is not the only source for appropriate stories. Everyday-life experiences, whether real or imaginary, can form a rich context for sharing the faith with children. Dorothy Jean Furnish, whose book *Exploring the Bible with Children* should be required reading for every person who prepares children's sermons, says, "A teacher need not always deal with the Bible itself to be described as teaching biblically. Because the Bible is a witness to God's encounter with persons in their human situation, this is reason enough to consider life's experiences."[16]

Our goal is to help our children be prepared for life in the light of the faith story. This can take several forms:

1. Stories about the children themselves (my grandchildren love them)
2. Stories about children of similar ages, doing familiar things (getting lost, having birthdays, being afraid of the dark)

3. Episodes from children's fiction (*The Velveteen Rabbit, The Giving Tree*)
4. Special occasions (beginning school, a new baby, Mother's Day, Thanksgiving, Christmas)

Creating Awe and Wonder

As we think about the learning process, it is well to remember the primary goal stated in the second chapter: to create a moment of awe and wonder. A PBS special on early childhood education gave a marvelous illustration of how an Italian teacher of five-year-olds achieved this. He was taking them into a cave for their first experience of spelunking. He had carefully introduced them ahead of time to what they might experience, but it was not his information that created the mood of wonder. It was his attitude. His own excitement showed through; his sparkling eyes and eager voice communicated to them his own awe about what they were to experience. As the children descended into the cave, there was no fear, no anxiety, but a chorus of five-year-old voices murmuring "*Bella! Bella!* Beautiful! The many-colored crystals!" We are guides too, and our goal is to introduce children to the many-colored crystals in God's Word and to help them exclaim "*Bella!*" over God's love for them.

Although this is not an easy task in the short time allotted, it is not altogether impossible. Here are some suggestions about creating an atmosphere of awe and wonder.

As you meditate on the passage of scripture or story you will be using, ask yourself: What in this story is marvelous, wondrous, awesome? We don't have to reserve these adjectives for Advent and Easter alone. The daily miracle of God's love is a wonder, an awesome reality, very like the miracle of creation.

Let this sense of wonder be reflected in your voice. This does not mean solemnity. The Italian guide had a lilt of humor and energy in his voice and manner, but wonder was there too. It does mean, however, taking seriously what we are trying to convey, respecting the importance both of the hearers and of what is to be heard. The choice of the story is only one part of creating an atmosphere of wonderment. The attitude, voice, and manner of the storyteller also play important roles. Wonder includes the elements of surprise, admiration, triggered by the unexpected, the amazing, the incredible. If we are trying to arouse these feelings in children, we must first be in touch with them ourselves. Becoming as little children may mean opening ourselves once again to the "wow" in life. Does a starry night really move us? Are we still amazed by the marvelous intricacy of how our body works? Do we ever sniff flowers, touch feathers, rustle leaves, or feel awe over something "strange, unexpected, incredible" that has happened to us?

The very tone of one's voice can create a sense of awe, of hush, of wonder, as every good storyteller knows. If you feel wonderment yourself over something God has done, do not treat it flippantly or halfheartedly but let your sense of miracle and admiration spill over into your voice. Too many children's sermons settle for what is clever, cute, or folksy and lose the feeling of good old-fashioned reverence. This does not mean exchanging warmth for a sonorous holier-than-thou attitude, but it does mean being willing to show that you cherish the mystery of God's ways of working in the world, that you too are awed by the splendor of God's grace and glory, and that you can still feel amazement and awe over the unexplainable miracles of life.

Start with an experience, either a biblical one or one from daily life, and "wonder" about the question arising from that experience. Agnes Junkin Peery shows how to do it with this story based on Psalm 139:6, 13–16:

> David, the shepherd boy, sitting on a hill watching
> his sheep, thought much about what God had done.

God had made sheep with wool to keep them warm, birds with feathers to shed the rain, dogs with noses to smell out dangerous animals. As David thought about these things, he looked at his hand holding his flute. The joints worked perfectly. He thought of his own breath coming out of his own chest which made it possible for him to make sounds on the flute. And the music he made came from his own head, as did the thoughts which turned into songs on his tongue! How had God made possible all these things? And so he sang about his thoughts:

"I am fearfully and wonderfully made!"
(Psalm 139:14, KJV)
"Such knowledge is too wonderful for me!"
(Psalm 139:6, KJV)

When David began thinking about how all of this came to be, he said,

"God,
You created every part of me,
You put me together in my mother's womb.
You knew that I was there.
When my bones were being formed,
Carefully put together in my mother's womb,
When I was growing there in secret,
You knew I was there!"
(Psalm 139:13–16, TEV, slightly rearranged)

Look at your body as David did! What seems wonderful to you?

Your toes wiggle when your brain says, "Wiggle!" How does that happen?

If you had been making your own body, could you have thought that up?

Each finger, except your thumb, has three joints! Why?

Your eyelids cover your eyes and blink without your even thinking about them. Why?

Your tongue and lips form words which are thought up in your head and are given sound by your throat! How?

Let us bow our heads in prayer. Each one of you might like to thank God for some wonderful part of your body, for some wonderful thing your body can do.[17]

Marvel with the children over the wonders of the world around us . . . of things we can touch and see.

Let prayer be a time of expressing awe and "touching mystery"; it should be full of feeling, not shallow or perfunctory.

Tell stories that end with questions to think about rather than morals.

Use poetic speech. Children are often more attuned to it than adults. Many children's books have the rhythm of poetry. Read them to get ideas about how to phrase wonderment. An example of this is found in Alvin Tresselt's *I Saw the Sea Come In:*

> Across the moors, past the spicy wild roses . . .
> over a bank covered with whispering beach
>   grasses . . .
> slithering down through the slippery sand of a
>   sand dune . . .
> down went the little boy to the sea,
> just as a new tide started its journey up the broad
>   white beach.
> And nobody was there because the little boy was
>   the first one.[18]

There is also another reason to use poetry with children. James Britton, a lifetime student of language, states that for the child "poetry is a primer in which he discovers our pattern of culture," for "poetry embodies the values by which we live" and "in poetry the child does not understand the values but lives them."[19] Piaget discovered that a child is constantly re-creating the world in the light of his or her experience of it. Piaget saw this as a rational, logical process; Britton understands that it happens also through the intuitive discoveries the child makes through poetry that gives voice to fears and anxieties and enables the child to reflect on them and resolve them.

Remember that the deepest levels of our experience are emotional, not rational, and it is on these levels that we must try to reach children. They need help in experiencing these deep levels; they need encouragement to explore; they need the support of someone who cares enough to be their guide into the cave of many-colored crystals.

NINE

Capsule *Clues*

So what does it all come down to? All our understanding of worship, our perception of how children develop mentally and spiritually, our proper use of language and methods—how do we put it all together?

To summarize, I offer, in the form of an anagram, these Capsule clues.

C Is for Choreography

It should be clear by now: The premise of this book is that the children's sermon is not to be taken lightly. If it is to be an integral part of the liturgy, if it is to be a significant moment of awe and wonder, if it is worth doing at all, it should be carefully choreographed. This means paying attention to various considerations.

The sermon's place in the order of worship. One suggestion is to have the sermon follow a hymn of praise suitable for children and a prayer phrased in words they can understand. Another is to have it follow the reading of the scripture. The flow of the service should be considered, so the children's sermon is not an interruption but an integrated part of the liturgy.

How the children are summoned. The invitation to them

should be simple and dignified but warm. This is not a time for flippancy or clever asides to the adults. The tone set by the invitation can help determine whether this is to be a true moment of worship or just an amusing entertainment. A children's hymn may be played as the little ones gather. This is especially helpful in large churches where it sometimes takes a while for them to reach the front of the church.

Where the children sit. It is possible, of course, to have the children remain in their pews, but I agree with Joseph Bragg, who says that "the act of moving to their place helps develop a sense of ownership in the place and in worship."[1] They may sit in the first pews, on the platform steps, or even on the floor (depending on the formality of the church setting). If they do sit on the platform steps, the sermon-giver should be careful to sit at one side instead of in the middle. This helps children focus attention on the sermon-giver rather than on the congregation. The sermon-giver should take time to get them settled before beginning. This may mean corraling a few straying two- or three-year-olds.

The posture of the sermon-giver. This is very important. Coming away from the pulpit, sitting on the level of the children, holding a small child on your lap—all these gestures communicate to the children that this is their time and their space. When the sermon-giver remains standing, the opportunity for demonstrating warmth and closeness is diminished. Children often want to touch a minister's robe or stole, almost as if to see if the minister is real—or to see if the minister is God. Johanna Klink records the words of one six-year-old girl: "When the pastor preaches, God is preaching. Everybody says that because he's in church. When the pastor isn't in church and is talking on the street, he isn't God, but an ordinary man."[2] It's sometimes difficult for very young minds to remember that the sermon-giver is human all the time.

Body language speaks volumes. It is important to appear relaxed. If the sermon-giver is nervous, it will show and will affect the warmth of the occasion. As the saying goes, "Never let them see you sweat!" *The Directory of Masses with Children* of the Catholic Church uses three words to describe the gestures and actions of the priest leading children's worship: "dignity, clarity, and simplicity."[3] If we recognize that dignity does not mean stuffiness, these three words provide wonderful guidelines for the sermon-giver.

Finally, attention should be focused on the children, not on the congregation. Children are very special gifts of God. If they are truly cherished by the sermon-giver, they will know. If the sermon-giver concentrates on reaching out to them with love and concern, his or her nervousness will diminish. If the sermon-giver receives this opportunity as a precious trust, he or she can be used by God.

How the sermon is concluded. I feel very strongly that the *only* appropriate way to end a children's sermon is with a prayer. If this time has been a moment of worship, a brief one-sentence prayer provides a fitting end. This prayer can capture the essence of the sermon and can also remind the children to pray. Finishing up merely with the words "thank you" leaves something to be desired. We do not thank adults at the end of the adult sermon! Saying "thank you" to the children implies that they came down to the front as a favor to you personally, not for a special moment of worship. "Thank you" is often used as a transition phrase, as a way of announcing that the sermon is over. It is far better to say quietly after the prayer, "You may now return to your seats," and avoid the unnecessary ambiguity of "thank you."

A Is for Attitude

Paul Larose says children need four *A*'s: obviously, they need *answers* for their mental and spiritual needs, but for their emotional needs they need *approval, attention, and affection.*[4] The attitude of the sermon-giver is a prime factor in determining how well these emotional needs are met.

We have already seen how attitude is expressed in the

body language of the sermon-giver. There are other considerations as well.

The attitude of eager anticipation. Think of the children's sermon as gift, not burden. I have heard, more times than I can count, "The children's sermon is the hardest thing I have to do" or "I dread having to think up a children's sermon!" The difficulty and the dread often stem from lack of preparation and from the resentment of having to do something about which one is unsure and for which one feels unskilled. Even if time is short, this opportunity to relate to children in a special way is a privilege and deserves an attitude of anticipation and eagerness. The children should feel that the sermon-giver is glad to be there.

The attitude of attention. The sermon-giver's smile, warmth, words of greeting, and interest in the children's comments all demonstrate that the children are important and worth attention. This moment is for them. The sermon-giver should lean into their minds and spirits, engage them, listen to them, and take them seriously. The sermon is not for the adults, even if they do sometimes say they get more out of the children's sermon than anything else. The sermon-giver should give himself or herself completely to the children, even as Jesus did, in spite of the disciples' attitude of "Why bother?"

The attitude of approval. Paying attention is a part of this, but approval needs to be verbalized as well. Children's contributions to the discussion need to be affirmed. Dorothy Jean Furnish shows how to do this even if the child's concept is unlike our own: "We might respond, 'That's a new idea! I've never thought about it like that before. To me it means. . . .' Or, 'I used to think that, too. Now I think. . . .'⁵ Be quick with praise but avoid condescension. Eliminate put-downs. Remember that children's insights can be startling, poetic, and enlightening. Herman Sweet once said, "A child has a right to belong to this community. It is his rightful inheritance. But a child cannot be brought to it. He has to be accepted into it."⁶

The attitude of affection. Simply put, the sermon-giver should love children. If our children are to grow in faith, they must know love. They must experience acceptance. In these days, when so many stories of child abuse are surfacing, the urgency of providing a safe, caring community for children is heightened. Even in middle-class congregations, there will be abused and neglected children. The children's sermon provides an opportunity for the faith community to say over and over again, We care about you. Remember that although children may pay little attention to our words, they can intuit who we are and what we are really feeling. They need our genuine, consistent, steadfast love.

P Is for Preparation

One of the most serious problems with children's sermons is that they are not adequately prepared. When little thought is given to them, they become exercises in superficiality or banality, unless the sermon-giver is extremely gifted at extemporaneous speaking. Preparation should include the following elements.

Begin with God's Word. Your own study of the scripture should always be the starting point. Suggestions were made in chapter 7 about coordination of the children's sermon with the scripture for the day. Let the Word itself speak to you. "A message for children does not start with an object looking for a truth; it is a truth looking for a way to be proclaimed, understood, and used."[7] Do exegesis on the text; let its real meaning surface. Find the gold nugget to proclaim, even if it is just a word or a phrase. And don't take it out of context to make a point. Ask, What would interest children in this passage? What would they want to know?

Plan ahead. Do *not* decide on the children's sermon as you are arriving at the church on Sunday morning. One minister finds it advantageous to plan children's sermons a year ahead in order to coordinate them with lectionary readings and with seasons of the church year. Such careful planning allows you to think about how you will interpret texts well in advance. If you are going to use pictures or objects to illustrate the sermon, you will also have time to locate them. At the very least, follow Brant Baker's advice to start two days ahead. (See chapter 8.) Above all, such advance planning allows you to be sensitive to the workings of the Holy Spirit rather than relying on last-minute impulse.

Write it out. This is probably the most frequently omitted step in preparation. "Why," you ask, "do I have to write out something that's only five minutes long?" The reason is simple: Because you should give it the same careful attention as any other part of the liturgy. Writing it down helps you focus on the main point you wish to make and establishes a clear sense of how that point will be made. In the words of Jerry Jordan:

> Manuscripts cause me to be intentional in the *what* and *how* that is said to the children. This means choosing my words carefully (words children can relate to); checking the sequential flow (whether or not my thoughts logically connect); selecting the most meaningful illustrations (ones that are simple and direct); avoiding moralizing (omitting all those obligatory words); and gauging the length (approximately five to six minutes).[8]

However, after it is written out, it's more effective if the manuscript is left behind when you sit down with the children. One exception, of course, is if you are using a children's book, such as the *Read-Aloud Bible Stories* mentioned in the last chapter. And it doesn't hurt to practice aloud so you are sure of the time it takes.

Use sermons written by others. These books can be a great help if you are just beginning to do children's sermons. They suggest ideas and approaches and ways to interpret texts for children. Be sure, however, to follow some simple guidelines.

Select only those that are theologically sound and show an awareness of how children learn. Be aware that a lot of very inappropriate material is published under the guise of "children's sermons." The Bibliography includes an annotated list of useful books.

Adapt them to your own situation. Very few can stand alone, "as is." Take time to make them appropriate. Some of the best may be too long. Edit, shorten, strengthen, revise.

Make them your own. Leave the printed text behind. It's better to talk with the children using ideas from the printed text than to feed them something canned.

Let the printed material be a springboard for your own creativity.

S Is for Scripture

At the risk of seeming boringly repetitious, I will say it again: "Scripture should be the starting point." Even seasonal emphases such as Thanksgiving can be rooted in scripture. My experience of children's sermons is that this practice is not generally followed.

These moments are too precious to squander on the same ideas the children will be getting in secular nursery schools and kindergartens. A grounding in the faith begins with a scriptural foundation. Awe and wonder are richer and deeper when they spring from the revelation of God through Jesus Christ in the scripture. Help children to understand themselves and their experience of life through the age-old faith stories, as well as through contemporary experiences. We would do well to listen to Lucie Barber:

> One of the best ways to introduce little children to God and Jesus is through stories. The best resource for stories about God and Jesus is the Bible. Unfortunately, many parents have difficulty recognizing the Bible as a resource for stories, or, if they do recognize the Bible

as a resource, they fail to know how to use it. You can help the parents in your parish to recognize that the Bible is a resource. You can also show them how to use it with their little children.[9]

U Is for Understanding

Think about the children. What is the age range of the children you will be addressing? What are their special needs related to where they are in the developmental process? What do they need, emotionally, spiritually, and cognitively? What are they able to comprehend? What is going on in their lives? Are there special happenings of which you should be aware—a new baby, a death in the family? Is someone moving away? Are there newcomers? It's important to know general characteristics of young children, but it's also important to know specifics about the lives in your own congregation.

If you are out of touch with children on a day-to-day basis, take some time to watch children's TV shows or browse through the children's book section in the library or bookstore. It won't hurt to read a few books about how children experience faith, such as *Your Child and Religion* by Johanna L. Klink, *Children in the Worshiping Community* by David Ng and Virginia Thomas, *The Spiritual Needs of Children* by Judith Allen Shelly, *Exploring the Bible with Children* by Dorothy Jean Furnish, and *The Religious Education of Preschool Children* by Lucie W. Barber.

L Is for Language

Keep your language simple. Avoid complicated lead sentences. One suggestion is to put a strong verb and a concrete noun in the first sentence. "Look at the sun shining through our windows this morning!"

Take care to keep language inclusive. Instead of using gender-specific words, it is better to use "one" or "they." The

New Revised Standard Version of the Bible is a big help with inclusive language.

Use abstract language and symbolism sparingly and with great caution. If they are used at all, take care to select images appropriate to the children's experience.

To introduce new religious words, give definitions, relate the terms to the children's experience, give synonyms for them, and help the children pronounce the words.

E Is for Energy, Excitement, and Enthusiasm

The children's sermon is a marvelous opportunity. Not only can it provide windows to awe and wonder for young children, it can do the same for the sermon-giver. It can refresh, energize, and stimulate. It can spark excitement about the future of the church and the possibilities that lie ahead for its children. It can be an instrument of grace, of shared love, which not only says something profoundly important to the children but reminds the sermon-giver of the infinite possibilities of God's love and the wondrous ways of God's grace. It can be a way for the sermon-giver to show unabashed enthusiasm for God's Word and for the church and to spark that enthusiasm in the young. To be enthusiastic is, literally, to be "in God." The children's sermon, by freeing us from pontificating and intellectualizing, allows God to shine through in our enthusiasm.

Sophie Koulomzin sums it up:

When being with children, loving children, participating in their growth, is *for you* a channel of Grace, when you feel that your own personality becomes more and more real as you communicate with children . . . then the Lord's words about children—"of such is the Kingdom of Heaven"—have a special, personal meaning for you. . . . We can go through life as if the world were not created by God, as if Christ were not born, as if He did not die and did not rise from the dead. Our natures are lazy and unimaginative. Then, suddenly, we have to teach all this. We become the vehicles through which these events make their impact on a child's growing mind. It is indeed a stimulating experience to become a wire through which passes this powerful electric current.[10]

Vehicles, wires, spelunking guides . . . all of these images remind us that the task of sharing the faith with children demands our serious thought, our best creativity, our inspired imaginations, our humility, our enthusiasm. It may not always be an easy task, but the rewards are even more exciting than introducing a group of children to a cave of jeweled crystals.

Notes

Chapter One: The Children's Sermon,
Burden or Blessing?

1. W. Alan Smith, *Children Belong in Worship*, 50–55.

Chapter Two: The Worship Setting

1. Dee Horn, "Russian Orthodox Childhood," 60–61.
2. Paul H. Vieth, *Worship in Christian Education*, 24–25.
3. John E. Burkhart, *Worship*, 17.
4. James F. White, *New Forms of Worship*, 40.
5. Joseph H. Bragg, Jr., *Moments with Children in Worship*, 7.
6. Iris V. Cully, *Christian Worship and Church Education*, 33.
7. Burkhart, *Worship*, 37.
8. Robert Coles, *The Spiritual Life of Children*, 37.
9. Edward Robinson, *The Original Vision*, 28.
10. Vieth, *Worship in Christian Education*, 13–14.
11. James A. Carr, "The Children's Sermon: An Act of Worship for the Community of Faith," 14.
12. Cully, *Christian Worship,* 160.
13. *The Constitution of the Presbyterian Church (U.S.A.), Part II: Book of Order,* W-1.4007. (Louisville, Ky.: Office of the General Assembly, 1991.)
14. Burkhart, *Worship*, 29.

15. Sofia Cavalletti, *The Religious Potential of the Child*, 139.
16. Robinson, *Original Vision*, 74.
17. Ibid., 98.

Chapter Three: The Sermon as Instrument of Proclamation

1. Jerry M. Jordan, *Filling Up the Brown Bag*, 13–14.
2. Eldon Weisheit, *God's Word in a Child's World*, 10.
3. Iris V. Cully, *Christian Child Development*, 58.
4. Robert Coles, *The Spiritual Life of Children*, xvii.
5. John H. Westerhoff III, *Bringing Up Children in the Christian Faith*, 29.
6. Weisheit, *God's Word*, 12.
7. Brant D. Baker, *Let the Children Come*, 9.
8. Margie Morris, *Helping Children Feel at Home in Church*, 58.
9. Ted Lazicki, *Something for the Kids*, 22.
10. Westerhoff, *Bringing Up Children*, 36.

Chapter Four: How Children Think

1. David Elkind and Irving B. Weiner, *Development of the Child*, 102.
2. Donald Ratcliff, ed., *Handbook of Preschool Religious Education*, 9.
3. Ron Miner, *Come Sit with Me*, 43.
4. Lawrence O. Richards, *A Theology of Children's Ministry*, 101.
5. Ibid., 123–24.

Chapter Five: How Children Grow in Faith

1. Urban T. Holmes III, *Young Children and the Eucharist*, 22.
2. Lucie W. Barber, *The Religious Education of Preschool Children*, 128.
3. See Joseph H. Bragg, Jr., ed., *Moments with Children in Worship Through the Church Year*, 75.

4. David Elkind and Irving B. Weiner, *Development of the Child*, 271.

5. Adapted from Lawrence O. Richards, *A Theology of Children's Ministry*, 97.

6. David Steele, "Tears," 7.

7. Quoted in Kenneth E. Hyde, *Religion in Childhood and Adolescence*, 20.

8. James W. Fowler, *Stages of Faith*, 122–34.

9. Ibid., 135–50.

10. Sophia Lyon Fahs, *Today's Children and Yesterday's Heritage*, 53.

11. Arnold Gesell and Frances L. Ilg, *The Child from Five to Ten*, 26.

12. Quoted in Edward Robinson, *The Original Vision*, 55.

Chapter Six: The Spiritual Needs of Children

1. Ruth Robinson, "Spiritual Education in a World Without Religion," 140.

2. Sylvia Ashton-Warner, *Teacher*, 53.

3. John H. Westerhoff III, *Bringing Up Children in the Christian Faith*, 21.

4. John H. Westerhoff III, *Will Our Children Have Faith?* 89–90.

5. Westerhoff, *Bringing Up Children*, 26.

6. Judith A. Shelly, *The Spiritual Needs of Children*, 29.

7. Westerhoff, *Will Our Children Have Faith?* 60.

8. Karen Leslie, *Faith and Little Children*, 3.

9. Lucie W. Barber, *The Religious Education of Preschool Children*, 103.

10. Donald Ratcliff, ed., *Handbook of Preschool Religious Education*, 66–69.

11. Iris V. Cully, *Christian Child Development*, 31.

12. Ratcliff, *Handbook*, 61.

13. Kenneth E. Hyde, *Religion in Childhood and Adolescence*, 22.

14. Barber, *Religious Education*, 108.
15. Ratcliff, *Handbook*, 73.
16. Barber, *Religious Education*, 106.
17. Cully, *Christian Child Development*, 69.
18. Hyde, *Religion*, 82.
19. Ibid., 65.
20. Stan and Jan Berenstain, *How to Teach Your Children About God . . . Without Actually Scaring Them Out of Their Wits*, n.p.

Chapter Seven: Language and Symbolism

1. Jerry M. Jordan, *Filling Up the Brown Bag*, 11.
2. James A. Carr, "The Children's Sermon: An Act of Worship for the Community of Faith," 42.
3. Sally McFague, *Speaking in Parables*, 56.
4. Kenneth E. Hyde, *Religion in Childhood and Adolescence*, 122.
5. Sonja Stewart and Jerome Berryman, *Young Children and Worship*, 7–8.
6. Agnes Junkin Peery, *Let All the People*, 87, 205.
7. Iris V. Cully, *Christian Child Development*, 153.

Chapter Eight: The Shape of the Sermon

1. Quoted in Iris V. Cully, *Christian Child Development*, 129–34.
2. Ibid., 132.
3. Eldon Weisheit, *God's Word in a Child's World*, 30.
4. Ginny Ellis, unpublished manuscript, n.p., n.d.
5. Agnes Junkin Peery, *Let All the People*, 27.
6. Brant D. Baker, *Let the Children Come*, 14.
7. Ibid., 37, 38.
8. Betty McLaney, "Litany," 28.
9. Elizabeth J. Sandell, *Including Children in Worship*, 39–41.
10. Johanna L. Klink, *Your Child and Religion*, 216.
11. Naomi Ragen, *Jephte's Daughter*, 18–19.

12. Ella K. Lindvall, *Read-Aloud Bible Stories*, 113.
13. Jerry M. Jordan, *Filling Up the Brown Bag*, 21–22.
14. Paul A. Schreivogel, *Small Prayers for Small Children*, n.p.
15. Peter Morgan, *Story Weaving*, 93, italics added.
16. Dorothy Jean Furnish, *Exploring the Bible with Children*, 89.
17. Peery, *Let All the People*, 313–14.
18. Alvin R. Tresselt, *I Saw the Sea Come In*, n.p.
19. James Britton, *Prospect and Retrospect*, 19.

Chapter Nine: Capsule Clues

1. Joseph H. Bragg, Jr., ed., *Moments with Children in Worship Throughout the Church Year*, 7.
2. Johanna L. Klink, *Your Child and Religion*, 2.
3. Paul Larose, *Working with Children and the Liturgy*, 23.
4. Ibid., 9.
5. Dorothy Jean Furnish, *Exploring the Bible with Children*, 108–9.
6. Quoted in Klink, *Your Child and Religion*, 212.
7. Eldon Weisheit, *God's Word in a Child's World*, 23.
8. Jerry M. Jordan, *Filling Up the Brown Bag*, 68.
9. Lucie W. Barber, *The Religious Education of Preschool Children*, 85.
10. Sophie Koulomzin, *Our Church and Our Children*, 128–30.

Bibliography

Ashton-Warner, Sylvia. *Teacher.* New York: Bantam Books, 1963.

Baker, Brant D. *Let the Children Come: A New Approach to Children's Sermons.* Minneapolis: Augsburg, 1991. A guide to "experiential" children's sermons. Acting out, using imagination. Brief introduction and samples. Ambitious but effective.

Barber, Lucie W. *The Religious Education of Preschool Children.* Birmingham, Ala.: Religious Education Press, 1981.

Berenstain, Stan and Jan. *How to Teach Your Children About God . . . Without Actually Scaring Them Out of Their Wits.* New York: Ballantine Books, 1971.

Bragg, Joseph. H., Jr., ed. *Moments with Children in Worship Through the Church Year.* St. Louis: CBP Press, 1989. A collection of excellent children's sermons based on the church year.

Britton, James. *Prospect and Retrospect: Selected Essays of James Britton.* Ed. by Gordon M. Pradl. Montclair, N.J.: Boynton Cook Publishers, 1982.

Brown, Carolyn C. *Forbid Them Not: Involving Children in Sunday Worship.* Based on the Common Lectionary, Years A, B, C. 3 vols. Nashville: Abingdon Press, 1991–93.

Burkhart, John E. *Worship.* Philadelphia: Westminster Press, 1982.

Carr, James A. "The Children's Sermon: An Act of Worship for the Community of Faith." *Perkins School of Theology Journal* 36, no. 3 (1983): 1–55.

Cavalletti, Sofia. *The Religious Potential of the Child.* New York: Paulist Press, 1982.

Coles, Robert. *The Spiritual Life of Children.* Boston: Houghton Mifflin Co., 1990.

Cully, Iris V. *Christian Worship and Church Education.* Philadelphia: Westminster Press, 1967.

———. *Christian Child Development.* San Francisco: Harper & Row, 1979. A very basic book applying learning theory to religious development.

Curran, Dolores. *Who, Me Teach My Child Religion?* Rev. ed. Minneapolis: Winston Press, 1981.

Elkind, David. *Children and Adolescents: Interpretive Essays on Jean Piaget.* New York: Oxford University Press, 1970.

——— and Irving B. Weiner. *Development of the Child.* New York: John Wiley & Sons, 1978.

Evans, Richard I. *Jean Piaget: The Man and His Ideas.* Tr. by Eleanor Duckworth. New York: E. P. Dutton & Co., 1973.

Fahs, Sophia Lyon. *Today's Children and Yesterday's Heritage.* Boston: Beacon Press, 1952.

Fowler, James W. *Stages of Faith: The Psychology of Human Development and the Quest for Meaning.* San Francisco: Harper & Row, 1981.

Furnish, Dorothy Jean. *Exploring the Bible with Children.* Nashville: Abingdon Press, 1975.

Gesell, Arnold, and Frances L. Ilg. *The Child from Five to Ten.* New York: Harper & Brothers, 1940.

Goldman, Ronald. *Readiness for Religion.* London: Routledge & Kegan Paul, 1965.

Hanson, Richard S. *Worshiping with the Child.* Nashville: Abingdon Press, 1988. Helpful guide to how children worship, using the Bible to involve children in worship and creating moments of awe and wonder. Poetic and practical.

Hendricks, William L. *A Theology for Children.* Nashville: Broadman Press, 1980.

Holmes, Urban T., III. *Young Children and the Eucharist.* Rev. ed. New York: Seabury Press, 1982.

Horn, Dee. "Russian Orthodox Childhood." *Alive Now* 18, no. 4 (July-August 1988): 60–61.

Hyde, Kenneth E. *Religion in Childhood and Adolescence: A*

Comprehensive Review of the Research. Birmingham, Ala.: Religious Education Press, 1990.

Jordan, Jerry M. *Filling Up the Brown Bag: A Children's Sermon How-to Book.* New York: Pilgrim Press, 1987. Exuberant, readable, sound approach to preparation of children's sermons, except for too much reliance on object lessons.

Klink, Johanna L. *Your Child and Religion.* Richmond: John Knox Press, 1972.

Koulomzin, Sophie. *Our Church and Our Children.* Crestwood, N.Y.: St. Vladimir's Seminary Press, 1975.

Larose, Paul. *Working with Children and the Liturgy.* New York: Alba House, 1981.

Lazicki, Ted. *Something for the Kids.* Ed. by Arthur L. Zapel. Colorado Springs: Meriwether Publishing, 1985.

———. *Where Does God Live? Fifty-eight More "Something for the Kids" Children's Sermons for Worship.* Ed. by Arthur L. Zapel and Rhonda Wray. Colorado Springs: Meriwether Publishing, 1991.

Leslie, Karen. *Faith and Little Children: A Guide for Parents and Teachers.* Mystic, Conn.: Twenty-Third Publications, 1990.

Lewis, C. S. *The Lion, the Witch and the Wardrobe.* New York: Macmillan & Co., 1950.

Lindvall, Ella K. *Read-Aloud Bible Stories.* Vol. 1. Chicago: Moody Press, 1982. Very well told Bible stories that provide good models for simple language use with children.

Lou, Sue; Jean Floyd Love; Mickey Meyers; and Sylvia Washer. *Get Ready! Get Set! Worship!* Houston: Sharing Tree Publications, 1992. A notebook of helpful ideas for educating children about worship and including them in worship.

McFague, Sallie. *Speaking in Parables: A Study in Metaphor and Theology.* Philadelphia: Fortress Press, 1975.

McLaney, Betty. "Litany." *Living the Word, Children's Book.* Level 3, Ages 4–5/5–6. Norcross, Ga.: General Assembly Mission Board, Presbyterian Church (U.S.A.), 1983.

Miller, Karen. *Ages and Stages: Developmental Descriptions and Activities—Birth Through Eight Years.* Marshfield, Mass.: Telshare Publishing Co., 1985.

Miner, Ron. *Come Sit with Me: Sermons for Children.* New York: Pilgrim Press, 1981.

Morgan, Peter. *Story Weaving: Using Stories to Transform Your Congregation.* St. Louis: CBP Press, 1986.

Morris, Margie. *Helping Children Feel at Home in Church.* Nashville: Discipleship Resources, 1988. Contains practical suggestions for parents, families and church workers on helping children learn how to worship.

Ng, David, and Virginia Thomas. *Children in the Worshiping Community.* Atlanta: John Knox Press, 1981. A landmark work on incorporating children into the total worship life of the congregation.

Old, Hughes Oliphant. *Worship.* Atlanta: John Knox Press, 1984.

Paterson, Katherine. *Bridge to Terabithia.* New York: Harper & Row, 1987.

Peery, Agnes Junkin. *Let All the People.* Richmond: Outlook Book Service, 1988. Excellent "story-conversations" based on the three year cycle of the church calendar, as well as special subjects such as the church, the sacraments, Hebrew customs and celebrations, stewardship, peacemaking, etc.

Piaget, Jean. *Play, Dreams, and Imitation in Childhood.* Translated by C. Gattegno and V. M. Hodgson. New York: W. W. Norton & Co., 1962.

——— and Bärbel Inhelder. *The Psychology of the Child.* Translated by Helen Weaver. New York: Basic Books, 1969.

Ragen, Naomi. *Jephte's Daughter.* New York: Warner Books, 1989.

Ratcliff, Donald., ed. *Handbook of Preschool Religious Education* Birmingham, Ala.: Religious Education Press, 1988.

Richards, Lawrence O. *A Theology of Children's Ministry.* Grand Rapids: Zondervan Publishing House, 1983.

Robinson, Edward. *The Original Vision: A Study of the Religious Experience of Childhood.* New York: Seabury Press, 1983.

Robinson, John A. T. *The New Reformation?* Philadelphia: Westminster Press, 1965.

Robinson, Ruth. "Spiritual Education in a World Without Religion." pp. 123–40 in John A. T. Robinson, *The New Reformation?*

Rowen, Betty. *The Children We See: An Observational Approach to Child Study.* New York: Holt, Rinehart & Winston, 1973.

Sandell, Elizabeth J. *Including Children in Worship.* Minneapolis: Augsburg, 1991.

Schreivogel, Paul A., *Small Prayers for Small Children.* Minneapolis: Augsburg Publishing House, 1980.

————. *More Prayers for Small Children: About Big and Little Things.* Minneapolis: Augsburg, 1988.

Shelly, Judith A. *The Spiritual Needs of Children.* Downers Grove, Ill.: InterVarsity Press, 1982.

Smith, Judy Gattis. *Come, Children, Praise and Pray.* Lima, Ohio: CSS Publishing Co., 1977.

————. "Activities to Develop Spiritual Growth in Children." *Church Teachers* 20, no. 4 (Jan.-Feb. 1993): 128–29.

Smith, W. Alan. *Children Belong in Worship: A Guide to the Children's Sermon.* St. Louis: CBP Press, 1984.

Steele, David. "Tears." *Presbyterian Outlook* 173, no. 35 (Oct. 14, 1991): 7.

Stewart, Sonja M., and Jerome W. Berryman. *Young Children and Worship.* Louisville, Ky.: Westminster/John Knox Press, 1989.

Tresselt, Alvin R. *I Saw the Sea Come In.* New York: Lothrop, Lee & Shepard Co., 1954.

Vieth, Paul H. *Worship in Christian Education.* Philadelphia: United Church Press, 1965.

Weaver, Andrew. "Children's Sermons Are Fun." *Christian Ministry* 10, no. 4 (July 1979): 23.

Weisheit, Eldon. *God's Word in a Child's World.* Minneapolis: Augsburg Publishing House, 1986.

Westerhoff, John H., III. *Bringing Up Children in the Christian Faith.* San Francisco: Harper & Row, 1984. Designed for parents. Excellent tool for understanding the basics of teaching the faith to children.

————. *Will Our Children Have Faith?* San Francisco: Harper & Row, 1983.

White, James F. *New Forms of Worship.* Nashville: Abingdon Press, 1971.

Printed in the United States
24598LVS00001B/196-219

9 780664 254391